NOAH'S FLOOD, JOSHUA'S LONG DAY, AND LUCIFER'S FALL

—What *Really* Happened?

By

RALPH WOODROW

A complete catalog of books and/or information
can be obtained by contacting:

RALPH WOODROW
P. O. BOX 21
PALM SPRINGS, CA 92263-0021

24-hour Phone Order/Message Line: (760) 323-9882
Toll-free (within the 48 states): (877) 664-1549
Fax: (760) 323-3982
E-mail: ralphwoodrow@earthlink.net
Web Site: www.ralphwoodrow.org

NOAH'S FLOOD, JOSHUA'S LONG DAY, AND LUCIFER'S FALL

Copyright © 1984 Ralph Woodrow Evangelistic Association, Inc.

P.O. Box 21, Palm Springs, CA 92263-0021

Third Printing, May 2000

International Standard Book Number: 0-916938-07-7

Library of Congress Card Number: 83-91482

INTRODUCTION

NOAH'S FLOOD...

When I first heard the idea that Noah's flood may have been a regional, rather than an absolutely worldwide flood, I paid little attention. After all, didn't the Bible say the flood covered all the mountains of the earth? Then around 1970, I was holding meetings at a church in Spearfish, South Dakota. One day, as the pastor and I were talking, he mentioned some weighty arguments in favor of the regional flood viewpoint that had been presented in a lecture series he attended while in Bible College. This was a strong Bible-believing, conservative, and evangelical school, certainly not one given over to modernism or liberalism. Though the pastor mentioned these things in passing, a seed was planted which caused me to pursue a detailed study over the next few years. Ultimately this information became part one of this book.

I am well aware there are some who feel an absolutely worldwide flood is nearly an "essential" of the Christian faith. I also realize that regardless of which position one takes, some unanswered questions remain. Without claiming to have the "final word" or "ultimate revelation" on the subject, I present what is written here *as a study,* perfectly content to let every person be fully persuaded in his own mind (Rom. 14:5).

JOSHUA'S LONG DAY...

There is also, I came to realize, an alternate explanation about Joshua commanding the sun to stand still. It is commonly believed that Joshua needed additional hours of daylight to defeat the Amorites, so he commanded the sun to stand still, the cycle of day and night was interrupted, and that day was extended for nearly 24 additional hours! *But* the Bible implies the cycle of day and night has *never* been interrupted (Jer. 33:20). We know, also, that the length of a day is not determined by the movement of the *sun*, but by the *earth* turning on its axis. The issue, then, centers on *how* we reconcile these things with the Biblical passage about Joshua commanding the sun to stand still.

The Hebrew word translated "stand still" doubtless means STOP. But did Joshua want the sun to stop *moving* (as commonly assumed) or to stop *shining?* As I studied this out, there were reasons to believe Joshua did not want a *longer* day, but *relief* from the heat of the scorching summer sun. If so, this would explain why his command to the sun resulted in a dark, massive storm moving in—it stopped the sun from shining on them, provided relief from the heat, as well as dropping huge hailstones upon their Amorite enemies.

I heard that *Moody Monthly* magazine years ago had an article that would possibly confirm this explanation. I asked a friend who was living in Chicago, close to the Moody Bible Institute, to go there and find the article for me. He did, and the photocopy he sent did confirm this position to which my own studies had led.

LUCIFER'S FALL...

The common belief about Lucifer is that he was once an angel in Heaven; that he led the angels in their worship of God; that he had unequaled strength, wisdom and beauty. But then he rebelled against God, was cast out of Heaven, and became the Devil.

As a young preacher, holding revival meetings in Flagstaff, Arizona, one night I echoed some of this teaching. I made the statement that the "first" sin was not that of Adam and Eve, but of Lucifer who rebelled against God and was cast out of Heaven. Afterward, a pastor told me he had a booklet in his library that said the passage about Lucifer (Isaiah 14) referred to the king of Babylon—*not Satan.* I was somewhat shocked, at the time, to hear that anyone held a different belief on this! Didn't *everyone* believe "Lucifer" was simply another name for Satan?

But in time I would come to realize this belief—at best a theory—is not actually spelled out in Scripture. As a note in the Amplified Bible says: "Some students feel that the application of the name Lucifer to Satan, in spite of the long and confident teaching to that effect, is *erroneous....* The application of the name has [only] existed *since the third century A.D. "* (Note on Isaiah 14:12).

Adam Clarke, a highly regarded Bible commentator, writing over a century and a half ago, said: "The truth is, the text [Isaiah 14] speaks nothing at all concerning Satan nor his fall, nor the occasion of that fall....This chapter speaks not of the ambition and fall of Satan, but of the pride, arrogance, and fall of Nebuchadnezzar [king of Babylon]." Make no mistake, we accept everything the Bible says about Satan. But we would caution against forming conclusions about his origin based on passages that describe the king of Tyrus and the king of Babylon (Ezekiel 28; Isaiah 14).

Having put considerable time into the three studies mentioned here, they eventually came together as: **NOAH'S FLOOD, JOSHUA'S LONG DAY, AND LUCIFER'S FALL.** Now, as I write this introduction for the third printing of this book, may I assure every reader I have no quarrel with any who may see some of these things differently. I am well aware there are details we may never fully understand until that Day when we are forever in the presence of Him who is himself Truth, Jesus Christ.

—RALPH WOODROW

CONTENTS

1

WAS THE FLOOD UNIVERSAL?

Most of us have heard the story about Noah and the ark from childhood. We took it for granted that the flood was universal, covering the highest mountains on earth, and that the only survivors were Noah, his family, and a host of animals: elephants, lions, giraffes, monkeys, horses, cows, dogs, cats, lizards, snakes, birds, and bees! The basic story is known by billions of people. It is included in the sacred writings of Christians, Jews, and Muslims. Nevertheless, what has been generally believed about the flood may not be what *really* happened!

Was the flood universal, covering the entire world? Or was it regional, involving human and animal life in one specific land? There are, of course, dedicated Christians on each side of this question, and each side has its able defenders, arguments, strengths, and weaknesses. But when all the evidence is in, we believe the bulk of the evidence favors Noah's flood as being REGIONAL, *not universal*.

If the flood was universal, every animal on earth today would have descended from those in the ark. This raises questions, of course, as to how this many animals would be able to fit into Noah's ark, how they were able to cross vast continents to get to the ark, and how they managed, after the flood, to get back home.

Right now as I write this in California, not too far away

there are some snails among the plants. These creatures move very slowly, having a top speed of 0.03 miles per hour. If the flood occurred less than 4,500 years ago (in 2,348 B.C., according to Ussher), would this even allow enough *time* for them to travel all the way from the mountains of Ararat to California? Were they able to cross oceans, ford rivers, bypass arctic zones, survive deserts, pass through jungles, climb mountains, and finally end up here? Such questions, as we will see, are only the tip of the iceberg as we face the implications of a world-wide flood.

Admittedly, as one reads the Genesis account in our English translation,* it does *seem* that the flood was nothing short of a world-wide, universal flood. It is described as,

*Unless indicated otherwise, all scripture quotations are from the King James Version.

6

A flood of waters upon the earth, to destroy all flesh, wherein is the breath of life, from under heaven; and every thing that is in the earth shall die (Genesis 6:17).

And, we read that when the flood came,

The waters prevailed exceedingly upon the earth; and all the high hills, that were under the whole heaven, were covered... and the mountains were covered. And all flesh died that moved upon the earth... Noah only remained alive, and they that were with him in the ark (Genesis 7:19-23).

Repeatedly we are told in the Biblical account that the flood would cover the *earth,* that everything in the *earth* would die, and other statements about the *earth,* all of which would teach the idea of a world-wide flood—*except for one thing: erets.*

Erets (number 776 in *Strong's Concordance*[1]), the Hebrew word that is translated "earth" throughout the flood account, simply does not require a world-wide meaning! It is translated "country" (140 times) and "land" (1,476 times) in the Bible. Literally hundreds of references show that *erets* is used most often of *limited* land areas.

Compare, for example, the way *erets* is used concerning Abraham. "Get thee out of thy *country* [*erets*]... unto a *land* [*erets*] that I will shew thee" (Genesis 12:1). If *erets* meant the earth as a planet, this would be like telling him to leave the earth and go to another planet! Later, "Abraham journeyed from thence toward the south *country* [*erets*], and dwelled between Kadesh and Shur" (Genesis 20:1). Obviously there was not a south planet earth as compared to a north planet!

Other references in Genesis also show that *erets* was used to designate specific lands: "the whole land [*erets*] of Havilah," "the whole land [*erets*] of Ethiopia," "the land [*erets*] of Nod, on the east of Eden," "the land [*erets*] of Shinar," "the land [*erets*] of Canaan," "the land [*erets*] of Egypt," "the Philistines' land [*erets*]," "the land [*erets*] of Moriah" (Genesis 2:11, 13, etc.). To substitute the word "earth" (as meaning the planet) in any of these references would be unthinkable.

Erets is used in the *plural*. We read of Gentiles "in their lands [*erets*]," of "enemies' lands [*erets*]," and of various nations called "lands [*erets*]" (Genesis 10:5; Lev. 26:36; 2 Kings 19:11, 17; etc.). The word "every" is used with *erets:* "I will get them praise and fame in every land [*erets*] where they have been put to shame" (Zeph. 3:19). If *erets* meant the planet earth, then the plural would be talking about planets—reducing the whole thing to absurdity!

Famine at the time of Joseph affected "all lands [*erets*]" (Genesis 41:54). When the storehouses were opened in Egypt, "all countries [*erets*]" came to buy corn (verse 57). It would be silly to read this as though all planets suffered from famines and came to Egypt to buy corn!

During the plagues upon Egypt, at one point we read that "the rain was not poured upon the earth [*erets*]" (Exodus 9:33). Everyone understands *erets* here to mean "land"—the land of Egypt. Why, then, in reading that "the waters of the flood were upon the earth [*erets*]" or that "the rain was upon the earth [*erets*]" (Genesis 7:10, 12) should we assume the whole planet is meant? The *erets* destroyed by the flood was the land in which Noah lived. Just how much land, or how far the flood extended, is not defined by this word.

THE FACE OF THE EARTH

During another plague upon Egypt, swarms of locusts were to "cover the face of the earth [*erets*], that one cannot

8

be able to see the earth...They covered the face of the whole earth [*erets*]...through all the land of Egypt" (Exodus 10:5, 14, 15). All recognize this destruction as pertaining to one land: Egypt. Why, then, should any insist that the flood covering "the face of the whole earth [*erets*]" (Genesis 8:9) must mean a universal flood? It is the same wording in both cases.

Having escaped from Egypt, the Israelites were described as "a people...which covered the face of the earth [*erets*]" (Numbers 22:5, 11). They covered enough land area for Balak to consider them a military threat to his tribe, but they obviously did not cover the entire planet! Vast quantities of quail fell upon "the face of the earth [*erets*]...a day's journey on this side, and as it were a day's journey on the other side round about the camp" (Numbers 11:31). The "face of the earth" in this passage was only a few square miles of land!

Twenty thousand men were killed in a forested area of Ephraim. Though this was a relatively small area, we are told that the battle was "scattered over the face of all the country [*erets*]" (2 Samuel 18:8). The word "country" appears here in the King James Version—and this is obviously the correct meaning—but it is exactly the *same* word that is used in the flood story about the waters being upon "the face of all the earth [*erets*]" (Genesis 7:3, 4).

Jeremiah once spoke of a flood overflowing the *erets,* and though he used "flood" to figuratively describe an invading army, it provides an interesting comparison: "Behold, waters rise up out of the north, and shall be an overflowing flood, and shall overflow the land [*erets*], and all that is therein; the city, and them that dwell therein: then the men shall cry, and *all* the inhabitants of the land [*erets*] shall howl" (Jeremiah 47:2). If, in this passage, we were to translate *erets* as it has been translated in the Genesis flood story, it would read: "A flood shall overflow the *earth* and all the inhabitants of the *earth.*" Surely wording this strong would seem to indicate a world-wide flood, yet the reference in Jeremiah only involved the land [*erets*] of the *Philistines*!

After Joshua had led the Israelites into the promised land, we read: "So Joshua took the *whole* land [*erets*] . . . and the land [*erets*] rested from war" (Joshua 11:23). No one would think of reading "earth" into this passage! Everyone knows that the conquest of Canaan did not include America, China, and Australia!

On and on, reference after reference, could be given in which *erets* is translated "earth," "country," "ground," or "land" — unmistakably used of limited land areas. With this point in mind, looking again at the expressions used to describe the flood, we read "land" as the correct meaning of *erets:* "the *land* was corrupt," "all flesh had corrupted his way upon the *land,*" "the waters of the flood were upon the *land,*" "all flesh died that moved upon the *land,*" "the waters returned from off the *land,*" etc. This puts a different slant on the whole thing. Once *erets* is understood, instead of the flood covering the entire planet, we can visualize it as a vast flood involving, primarily, the land in that part of the world in which Noah lived.

INTERNAL EVIDENCE

Even without comparing the way *erets* is used in *other* verses, there is internal evidence for the same conclusion *within the flood account itself.* Consider, for example, the *reason* for the flood: ". . . the earth [*erets* — *land*] was filled with violence" (Genesis 6:11). "Land" is correct, for violence could only occur where there were *people* to cause the violence. Since large portions of the world were uninhabited at this point in human history, it was not the planet earth

10

that was filled with violence, but the land — the land in which Noah lived.

We read also that "the waters increased, and bare up the ark, and it was lift up above the earth [*erets — land*]" (Genesis 7:17). Again, we read "land" for *erets,* for this gives a more accurate picture than supposing the ark was lifted above the planet!

It is generally understood that after the forty days of rain, the flood still "prevailed" or maintained its level for a period of time before abating (Genesis 7:24). If the waters of the flood prevailed upon the "land" in which Noah lived — and not the entire planet — there would have still been streams draining down from higher elevations. This could have maintained the level of the flood for a period of time, even though it had stopped raining. But if the flood covered the entire world, where would the waters come from to maintain this level after the rain had stopped?

Later, "God made a wind to pass over the earth [*erets — land*]" and the waters receded (Genesis 8:1). A wind passing over a body of water picks up moisture, forming clouds which move with the wind to drop rain in other areas. But if the whole planet was covered with water, moisture-laden clouds passing on to rain somewhere else would have only dumped water on more water! This would be like dipping water out of one end of a swimming pool and pouring it in the other end — the level would remain unchanged! But if we understand the flood as being in a certain region, then a wind passing over could carry away moisture to some dry and distant land. This would cause a lowering of the waters as the scriptures describe.

"And the waters returned from off the earth [*erets — land*] continually" (Genesis 8:3). We can picture water draining down from the land of Ararat and through Meso-

The Dove Sent Forth From the Ark—Gustave Doré

potamia into the Persian Gulf—returning from off the *land*. But if the *planet* earth was meant, and waters drained off *it*, where did they drain to?

Finally, "the waters were dried up from off the earth [*erets—land*]" (Genesis 8:13). Since 71 percent of the earth's surface is water, if the entire earth was meant, the waters drying up from off the earth would even include the oceans! But with the reading that the water dried up from off the *land*, language is allowed to retain its normal flow of thought, showing that the land that was flooded had now dried up again.

UNDER THE WHOLE HEAVEN

But what about the statement in the flood account that all the mountains under the *whole* heaven were covered? "And the waters prevailed exceedingly upon the earth [*erets*]; and all the high hills, that were *under the whole heaven,* were covered. Fifteen cubits upward did the waters prevail; and the mountains were covered" (Genesis 7:19, 20). Would not this indicate that the flood was absolutely universal? No; not necessarily, for the expression "under the whole heaven" is often used in a limited way. The same wording in Deuteronomy 2:25: "...the nations which are *under the whole heaven,*" is limited by the context to a few Canaanite tribes in one small part of the world.

The people who overthrew Babylon—"the Medes"— came "from a far country, from the end of heaven" (Isaiah 13:5, 7). "The end of heaven" was a figure of speech used to designate a country beyond the distant horizon. Cities that were "walled up to heaven" (Deut. 1:28) did not have walls that literally touched the sky any more than our modern "skyscrapers" scrape the sky! In all of these instances, the use of the word heaven is limited by the context. A strict literalism is out of place.

The expression about all the high hills "under the whole heaven" is best understood as *all hills a person might see from one place*—from horizon to horizon. There is no reason to suppose this included hills thousands of miles away on the other side of the planet!

If all hills and mountains in the *world* were covered by the flood—as with the universal flood viewpoint—this would place the level of the flood fifteen cubits above Mount Everest, the highest mountain in the world! We do not believe this was the meaning intended by the writer of Genesis. Scripturally, it will not fit. Notice the *order* of events in Genesis 8:4, 5:

> And the ark rested in the seventh month, on the seventeenth day of the month, upon the mountains of Ararat. And the waters decreased continually until the tenth month, on the first day of the month, were the tops of the mountains seen.

It was 74 days *after* the ark rested that "the tops of the mountains were seen." We believe these were some mountains right around the spot where the ark came to rest. If the writer meant all the mountains in the world, he should have said the tops of the mountains were seen and *after* this the ark rested on the mountains of Ararat. This is self-evident, for there are *mountains all over the world that are higher than any in that land that was anciently known as Ararat!*

Even if we were to grant that the ark rested on the *highest* mountain in Ararat—at 16,946 feet—if all the mountains in the *world* were covered by the flood, as the water level went back down, many mountain tops would have become visible *before* this. Mount Everest, at an elevation of 29,028 feet, would have been first. In Africa, there would have been Mount Kilimanjaro at 19,340 feet; in Canada, Mount Logan at 19,850 feet; in Alaska, Mount McKinley at 20,320 feet; in Russia, Mount El'brus at 18,482 feet; in Argentina, Mount Aconcagua at 23,035 feet; in Mexico, Mount Citlaltepetl at 18,700 feet, etc. It is evident, then, that the writer of Genesis was speaking only of hills or mountains in one certain area being covered by the flood.

Ten highest mountains in the world (all over 26,000 feet) compared to the highest mountain in Ararat (16,946 feet).

Or to put it another way, since it was not until *after* the ark rested that the tops of the mountains were "seen," if the Genesis writer meant mountains world-wide, we would be driven to the absurdity that the ark was under no less than TWO MILES of water when it came to rest! And this would be granting that it rested on the very highest mountain in Ararat. Unless we are ready to say the ark was a submarine, the mountains mentioned in Genesis that were covered by the flood and were later seen after the flood, must be *local* mountains, not all mountains in the world!

WATER FROM WHERE?

If the flood covered every mountain on earth, where did this amount of water come from? And what became of the water when the flood subsided? Even *The Genesis Flood,* a book written to defend the universal flood concept, admits:

A global rain continuing for forty days, as described in the Bible, would have required a completely different mechanism for its production than is available at the present day. *If all*

15

the water in our present atmosphere were suddenly precipitated, it would only suffice to cover the ground to an average depth of *less than two inches.*[2]

If the flood covered all mountains on earth, we are looking at an average depth of over FIVE MILES of water that would be required. Needless to say, this is much more than "two inches." Continuing now to quote from *The Genesis Flood:*

> The process of evaporation could not have been effective during the rain, of course, since the atmosphere immediately above the earth was already at saturation level. The normal hydrologic cycle would, therefore, have been incapable of supplying the tremendous amounts of rain the Bible record describes.[3]

Once we recognize that the flood was regional, however, and not universal, this whole problem is brought back down to size.

In order to get a better idea of just how much water would be involved in a universal flood, consider the following: Since Mount Everest is 29,028 feet, a flood fifteen cubits above this, would be about 29,050 feet of water above normal sea level. It rained forty days and nights, so this would work out to roughly 726 feet of rain a day! Thirty feet an hour! Six inches of rain per minute! An inch of rain every ten seconds!

Twice I have visited Mount Waialeale in Hawaii which has the highest average rainfall of any spot on earth — 460 inches of rain a year. But, according to the above calculations, if the flood had been universal, it would have rained 8,712 inches a *day* — world-wide — over 18 times as much as Mount Waialeale receives in an entire *year!* This would be like living under a waterfall. Had this happened, it seems to me the light of the sun and even air to breathe would have been cut off.

After it stopped raining and the water began to go back down, the Bible implies the water receded at the rate of 15 cubits in 74 days (Genesis 7:20; 8:4, 5). A number of recognized commentators have mentioned this point.[4] If we figure a cubit at about 18 inches, the water level would have dropped 270 inches during this time or, to round it off, 4 inches a day. If the flood depth was 29,050 feet (348,600 inches) and the water level dropped 4 inches a day, it would take 87,150 days to get back down to normal sea level. That would be almost 239 *years*! The whole time of the flood is normally figured at around a year in duration *certainly not 239 years*! All of this argues against the idea that the flood was thousands of feet in depth and strongly suggests, rather, that it was a flood of regional proportions.

2

ANIMALS AND OTHERS

When the animals gathered to go into the ark, did this include a pair of every single kind of animal in the world — as the universal flood would require? Did this gathering include giraffes from Africa, kangaroos from Australia, polar bears from Alaska, three-toed sloths from South America, and giant pandas from China?

Or,

Was it a gathering of animals within the *land* in which Noah lived, animals threatened with extinction from a vast flood *in that area*?

Again, we must notice the use of the word *erets.* The Bible says the flood was to come upon the earth [*erets — land*], to destroy all flesh...and every thing that is in the earth [*erets — land*] shall die." Consequently,

Giraffe

Noah was told to bring "two of every sort into the ark, to keep them alive. . . of fowls after their kind, and of cattle after their kind, of every creeping thing of the earth [*erets* —*land*] after his kind" (Genesis 6:17-20).

Admittedly, to our modern minds, the word "earth" in passages such as these seems to convey the idea that the whole planet was meant. But when we realize that *erets* more correctly means "land," that the animals guided to Noah were animals of the land area in which he lived, the amount of animals is lessened considerably. To suppose that the flood involved all the animals of the entire world poses problems that are insurmountable, as we feel the pages which follow will show.

First, there is the problem of *space* on the ark. The Bible gives the dimensions of the ark as 300 cubits long, 50 cubits wide, and 30 cubits high (Genesis 6:15). Figuring a cubit at 18 inches would make the ark 450 feet long, 75 feet wide, and 45 feet high. Apelles, a Christian who lived around A.D. 130, asked—as many others have asked over the centuries: Would an ark this size be large enough to provide room for pairs of all animals of the entire world—of every beast, fowl, and creeping thing?

How many animals are we talking about? Jan Lever, a Professor of Zoology at the Free University of Amsterdam, has written that if the flood was universal, "the *lowest* estimate of the number of animals in the ark *would be fully 2,500,000*"![1] The writers of *The Genesis Flood,* who seek to uphold the universal flood position, argue for a smaller number than this. Then they point out that a railroad stock car with two decks can haul 240 sheep, that about 522 of these cars would fit into the ark, and so a considerable number of animals could be packed into the ark. They conclude that all animals rescued from a world-wide flood could "easily" fit into the ark and that "a few simple calcu-

Artist's concept of animals entering the ark — J. James Tissot.

lations dispose of this *trivial objection* once and for all."[2]

There is no reason to question the sincerity of people who make such statements; after all, they feel they are upholding an orthodox position in a world of unbelievers and skeptics. I am certainly no expert in questions of zoology and it would be folly for me to even attempt a guess about how many animals would have been involved. But it seems to me that the space problem for all of these animals in the ark cannot be dismissed as merely a "trivial objection."

It is not necessary to go into great detail about the sizes of various animals — such information being generally known and available — but we will give a few brief statements. An African elephant 12 feet high may have tusks 10 feet long and weigh 7 tons! A rhinoceros may be 11 feet in length, not counting a main horn which may extend another 4 feet. A giraffe, the tallest living animal, reaches a height of about 20 feet. Needless to say, huge animals such as these would take up considerable room in the ark.

The crocodile averages 14 to 16 feet, but some are over 20 feet. Most lizards are small — there are some 3,000 species — but a lizard found on certain Indonesian islands averages about 8 feet in length! Some snakes are as thick as the human body and over 30 feet long. The giant tortoise, believed to live longer than any other animal, has a shell of 4 feet and weighs over 500 pounds. Armadillos range from the fairy armadillo (which is 5 inches long and spends most of its life underground) to the giant armadillo (which is 5 feet long and weighs 110 pounds).

Though some birds are quite small and would not take up too much space in cages, an ostrich stands 7 feet tall. A peacock, though not this tall, spreads it plumage out 7

Ostrich

21

feet *wide.* The wandering albatross of the southern oceans has an average wing span of over 10 feet.

I own a house on a lot slightly larger than 100 by 100 feet. All of the lots on my block are the same size. If we figure the area covered by 10 of these lots — my lot and those of nine neighbors — we have about the same total floor space as would have been on the ark, counting all three levels. The area of these lots would fit within a fence 318 feet by 318 feet. By no stretch of the imagination do I believe that a pair from every type of animal in the world would fit into this tiny space. Just imagine my neighbors moving into my house with me and our few lots becoming a corral for elephants, giraffes, horses, rats, foxes, buffalo, camels, dogs, cats, anteaters, alligators, snakes, lions, tigers, leopards, turtles, penguins, kangaroos, baboons, chickens, armadillos, iguanas, gila monsters, and many, many more for a year!

Armadillo

You see, it is not merely a question of how many sheep can be crammed into a railroad car on its way to the slaughterhouse. The animals on the ark needed space enough to move about and exercise. They needed to remain in good health to survive the flood and propagate their kind later. An African lion chases its prey at speeds of 40 to 50 miles an hour. A cheetah can run 60 miles an hour. Even

Lion

a bulky-looking, unstreamlined rhinoceros can charge with the speed of a race horse! Kangaroos have been known to jump as far as 42 feet. Some birds have been recorded at speeds of over 100 miles an hour. None of these creatures could be crammed into cages like sardines in a can and properly survive.

As we consider the problem of space on the ark, we must also bear in mind that Noah not only took *one* male and *one* female into the ark. In some cases he took *seven* males and *seven* females! "Of every clean beast thou shalt take to thee by sevens, the male and his female...of fowls also of the air by sevens, the male and the female" (Genesis 7:2, 3). "Seven pairs" is the wording of many translations and the obvious meaning, for Noah could not take three-and-a-half males and three-and-a-half females. This means, then, that the number of clean animals must be multiplied by 14!

Apparently the animals designated as "clean" were those that were clean for *sacrifices,* for after the flood Noah "took of every clean beast, and of every clean fowl, and offered burnt offerings on the altar" (Genesis 8:20). There were five kinds of animals considered clean for sacrifice in the Bible: cattle, goats, sheep, doves, and pigeons (Lev. 1, 5, etc.). If we consider the meaning of "clean" to also include those creatures that were clean to be *eaten* (Lev. 11; Deut. 14), the numbers on the ark mount even higher! These would include the partridge, peacock, pheasant, sparrow,

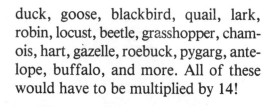

duck, goose, blackbird, quail, lark, robin, locust, beetle, grasshopper, chamois, hart, gazelle, roebuck, pygarg, antelope, buffalo, and more. All of these would have to be multiplied by 14!

Indian spotted deer

Hasting's Encyclopedia of Religion and Ethics, pointing out the "striking difficulties" of the universal flood idea, states that the ark would have been "infinitely too small to contain sevens of all clean animals, and pairs of unclean animals."[3]

The *Biblical, Theological, and Ecclesiastical Cyclopedia,* written almost 100 years ago, makes the same point: "Perhaps the most startling of all the difficulties in the way of the belief in a universal deluge are presented to us in the researches of the zoologist... the ark was totally inadequate to contain the animals even of a single continent... No vessel ever fashioned by man could have accommodated a tithe of these inmates."[4]

We are not told that Noah made any provision to keep each pair of animals separated on the ark, so there is the question of possible reproduction—and even more demands for space. In the accompanying cartoon, Captain Noah, with a somewhat forlorn look on his face, is about to have a talk with Mr. and Mrs. Rabbit. With an already crowded boat, he did not want additions! The basis for the cartoon is, of course, the fact that rabbits can reproduce rapidly. A female rabbit can bear 5 to 7 litters per year! Her gestation time is only 28 to 31 days. Within a matter of hours

*"I want to have a little talk with
you two in my cabin."*

AL JOHNS IN <u>REDBOOK</u>

after giving birth, she may mate again and be pregnant as
she raises the former litter. At this rate, the two rabbits
that entered the ark could have been the proud parents of
many rabbits by the time the flood was over!

Other animals that have a gestation period of *less* than
a year and who, consequently, could have given birth during
the time on the ark, include the following: bear (208 days),
cat (64 days), cow (280 days), dog (64 days), guinea pig
(68 days), hamster (16 days), lion (108 days), mouse (19
days), opossum (12 days), pig
(113 days), sheep (148 days),
tiger (110 days), etc. If all
of these animals reproduced
during the year on the ark,
more space, more food,
and more care would
be required!

Of course some may
suppose that in the

Great Kodiak bear

25

divine arrangement, no
reproduction took place
during the year the an-
imals were on the ark.
But if the flood was uni-
versal, reproduction *had to*
occur during that time for
the simple reason that

Chickadee

some creatures do not live a year! Unless these reproduced
during that time, none of their kind would have been alive
to reproduce after the flood was over!

According to *Life-Spans or How Long Things Last*,[5] a
worker bee lives 6 months and drones (males) about 8
weeks. Male ants die soon after mating and their life-span
may be as short as a few days. There are over 3,500 living
cockroach species. The large black cockroach that is commonly seen has a life-span of about 40 days. A common
field cricket has a life-span of 9 to 14 weeks. The common
housefly, only one of 85,000 fly species, has an average
life-span between 19 and 30 days, though there is a record
of an extremely sheltered fly that lived 70 days. Of the 9,000
different species of grasshoppers, the familiar green insect
we know by that name lives only 5 months. The desert
locust which migrates in vast herds across Africa and Asia
—and probably the locust mentioned in the Bible—has a
life-span of about 75 days. Mosquitoes coddled and nur-
tured in a laboratory have lived 5 months, but normally
live no longer than 2 months.

If the flood was
world-wide, repro-
duction on the ark
would have only
added to the already
impossible space

Crocodile

26

requirements. If the animals did not reproduce, how did those with a life-span of less than a year survive? How is it that they are in the world today? We believe the local flood position solves this dilemma.

If Noah's rescue mission involved every single type of creature in the world from huge reptiles to tiny insects — he would have had quite a task sorting them all out by "male" and "female"! This would require more knowledge than distinguishing between a bull and a cow. Did he know how to distinguish a male snake from a female snake? When he took two ants aboard, did he know how to choose one male and one female? Was he able to identify a male termite from a female termite? *Time* magazine once reported there are about 5 million species of insects. The problem of space for all of these on the ark would not be as great as that of sorting them out so there was one male and one female of each! Some creeping things are so tiny they are invisible. The problem is further complicated because some creatures, such as most land snails, have both male and female organs and, as such, are not individually male or female!

*   *   *

Water weevil

Leaf insect

Queen bee

Fruit fly

Termite

Sand-hopper

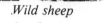

Problems for the universal flood become even more evident when we consider the tremendous amounts of *food* that would be required for all the animals. In addition to a male and female of every animal on earth — and seven males and seven females of some — we must remember that *many more* animals would have to be taken on the ark because *some animals survive by eating other animals.*

Wild sheep

Adam Clarke figured that one sheep would be sufficient meat for two wolves for three days. This works out to about 122 sheep for the year in the ark — 122 "extra" sheep just to feed two wolves! But we must remember that these sheep had to be fed until they were butchered to feed the wolves! The last sheep to be killed — we will call it "sheep number 122" — would have required food for almost the entire year. Just the grass or feed to sustain sheep — in order to sustain the two wolves — would have taken up considerable storage space.

The numbers count up even more when we consider that some animals eat animals, that eat animals, that eat animals! Suppose that during the last week of the year in the ark, one of the car-nivorious animals ate a

Great anteater

mongoose for lunch. At first glance this may seem of little consequence, but consider how much would have been involved in this one meal! The mongoose is well-known as a snake eater. For it to remain alive during the year on the ark, a supply of

Leopard

snakes would have been required. In order for these snakes to live until eaten by the mongoose, they would have required a supply of lizards to eat. In order for the lizards to live until eaten by the snakes, they would have required a supply of insects to eat. In order for the insects to live until eaten by the lizards, they would have required a supply of other insects to eat!

For every single meat-eating animal taken on the ark, *many more creatures would be involved*! Shrews kill and consume *twice* their own weight each day! A lion's favorite food is zebra. Leopards eat antelopes, monkeys, and are especially fond of domestic dogs. Cats eat birds. Birds eat worms. Anteaters eat termites. It is impossible to estimate how many extra zebras, antelopes, monkeys, dogs, birds, worms, and termites would be required for all the meat-eating animals!

Problems such as these have caused some who hold the universal flood viewpoint to suggest that Noah may have taken

Zebra

Horse

only small, baby animals on board! Of course there is not the slightest hint of this in scripture. Some have suggested that all the animals *hibernated* during the flood and, consequently, did not require food. But, again, this cannot be the case, for Noah was plainly told to take food for himself *and the animals* (Genesis 6:21).

Consider how much food this would be. An elephant will daily consume 44 pounds of grain, 66 pounds of hay, 20 to 70 pounds of turnips, carrots, cabbage or fruit. If an elephant eats 170 pounds of food each day, this would be 62,050 pounds during the year on the ark. Tons and tons of food! Picture the few pounds we carry home from the store in a grocery bag and compare this with over 62 *thousand* pounds of food! Think of the storage space this would take on the ark! Then, of course, since there would have been a male and a female elephant, we must double this amount, making a total of 124,100 pounds of food — over 62 *tons*. This much just for the two elephants on board!

Even for smaller animals, such as the common cow, the amount of food required counts up quickly. An average consumption for each cow would run about 20 pounds of hay and 50 pounds of silage per day; that would be

Cow

25,550 pounds for the year on the ark. But, we must not forget there were *fourteen* of these — 7 bulls and 7 cows — which would bring the total to a staggering 357,700 pounds of hay and silage! Imagine how long it would have taken just to get the ark *loaded* with such vast amounts of food before the rains came!

Llama

According to the Purebred Dairy Cattle score card, the desired weight for the black and white Holstein breed is 1,500 pounds for females and 2,000 pounds for males. Since there would have been seven of each of these on the ark, we are looking at a total weight of 24,500 pounds. Add this to the weight of the feed they would require for a total of 382,200 pounds—that is, over191 *tons!*

Though the diet of goats may range from woolen clothing to tin cans, many animals require a *specialized diet.* The giant panda of China is almost exclusively a bamboo-eater. The principle source of food for the giraffe is the acacia tree. The koala of Australia feeds exclusively on the leaves of a species of eucalyptus tree. The three-toed sloth, during its few waking hours, munches leaves of the cecropia tree. Obviously Noah did not travel to distant lands to get food for all of these

Camel

animals, another implication that the animals taken into the ark were only from the area in which he lived.

Even if all the tremendous food problems were solved, there would still be the question of *water* to drink. Unless some provision was made *inside* the ark, it would have been a case of "water, water everywhere, but not a drop to drink." It has been figured that about eight times the amount of water that is in all the oceans would be required to drown the world. If we take water in the same ratio — say eight quarts of fresh water and add one quart of water from the ocean — we no longer have water that would be very good to drink. As Custance has written: "A sufficient supply of water for drinking would probably have to be taken on board since the mingling of the waters in a world-wide flood would presumably render it unfit to drink."[6]

Gorilla

An elephant washes down his food with 30 to 50 gallons of water daily. Figuring 100 gallons for the two elephants on the ark, this would be 36,500 gallons of water for the year! An average size swimming pool — 15 feet by 30 feet — holds 16,875 gallons of water. The water requirements for just two elephants on the ark would

Elephants

more than fill two of these swimming pools! In weight, this would be 304,045 pounds of water (over 152 tons!), a gallon of water weighing 8.33 pounds. Imagine the tremendous

Rhinoceros

amount of water—and its weight—if every type of animal in the world was involved!

Even the comparatively smaller supply of drinking water that would be required for *people* on the ark counts up. If each person drank eight 10-ounce glasses of water per day, this would make a total of 5 gallons of water for the 8 people per day. Multiply this times 365 days for the year and we have 1,825 gallons. Picture the size of a gallon jug and then imagine 1,825 of these for drinking water—not to mention additional water that would be required for such things as washing clothes and bathing!

The average American eats around 1,351 pounds of food a year. This breaks down as follows: meat (165 pounds), poultry products (97 pounds), dairy products (288 pounds), fats and oils (55 pounds), fruits (224 pounds), vegetables (268 pounds), grains (129 pounds), and miscellaneous (125

Toucan

pounds).[7] Since there were 8 people on the ark, this would mean that a supply of food (if figured on this basis) would have amounted to 10,808 pounds!

If the flood was world-wide, clothing requirements would have ranged from very light clothing in the sultry plains

Dignity and impudence

of Mesopotamia to heavy coats for the extreme, freezing elevation to which the ark would have ascended. Changes of clothing would have been required, also bedding and bathroom articles. Times were more primitive back then, of course, but we should not suppose that food and water were the only necessities. Anyone leaving on a year long cruise, knowing there would be no ports en route, would certainly have to take quite an array of supplies. When these are considered, along with the food and water, a considerable amount of storage space would be required!

3

CARE AND CONCERN

Those of us who once assumed the flood was absolutely universal, simply did not stop to think of the tremendous amount of care this would involve. Custance has written:

It is rather difficult to visualize a flood of world-wide proportions but with so little turbulence that four men (perhaps helped by their womenfolk) were able to care for such a flock. It would take very little unsteadiness to make the larger animals almost unmanageable. It becomes even more difficult to conceive how proper provision could have been made for many animals which spend much of their time in the water, such as crocodiles, seals, and so forth.[1]

Safety bands for supporting cattle in rough sea.

Some creatures that could not survive a year in water, could not survive in a dry cage either. The white rhinoceros is so named because of its grayish-white appearance from wallowing in mud. Did Noah provide mud for these and many other animals to wade in? Some creatures, such as worms and moles, live underground. Were some areas of the ark filled with dirt for these? If all the different kinds of snakes were taken on the ark, how were they confined? They could not merely be put in cages like birds! On the other hand, if they were too tightly confined, there might be problems of access for feeding. In the accompanying drawing, first published in 1675 in Amsterdam, the artist shows rooms for the various animals and seeks to solve the snake problem by placing them on a separate level beneath all the rest!

Some animals such as sloths and koalas live in trees. Did Noah provide trees in some parts of the ark? Woodpeckers peck wood. Was extra wood supplied for them to peck so they would not make holes in the ark itself? Termites, also, would need a separate supply of wood! And, if all types of animals of the world were on the ark, imagine the job of cleaning the ark, removing the manure! Computations by some San Diego zoologists indicate that up to 800 tons of manure would have accumulated in the lower deck during the year aboard the ark.

Many animals survive only in certain climates. It is obvious that Noah did not heat one part of the ark for tropical animals and refrigerate another part for polar bears and penguins! Some animals survive only at certain elevations. But with the universal flood idea, animals would have had to survive through *a whole range of climates and elevations!*

17th century artist's concept of rooms for animals on lower floor

36

As the ark began to rise on the flood waters — if the flood was world-wide — all of these animals would have passed through every climate zone and elevation that any animal has ever lived in! Up, up, up with the level of the flood! Up from the hot plains a few feet above sea level to the cool mountain heights! Up still more to the level of peaks shrouded in perpetual snow and ice! Up until they were floating — or *freezing!* — in an ark at over 29,000 feet elevation, higher than Mount Everest, as high as we fly today in a 747 jet airplane! Fortunately for us in the airplane, though, the cabin is pressurized so we can breathe at such dizzy heights!

The Guiness Book of World Records says the highest altitude recorded for a bird is 27,000 feet. Some whooper swans flying from Iceland to the United Kingdom were spotted at this altitude by an airline pilot in 1967.[2] But with the idea that the flood covered the highest mountains in the world, we are asked to believe that every type of animal in the world went higher than birds have ever flown, in Noah's ark! Does anyone really believe that snakes, gophers, termites, elephants, iguanas, giraffes, and pairs of every single animal on earth today were in a boat at over 29,000 feet? J. Sidlow Baxter has written:

> Clearly, we are not intended to picture Noah and the ark as borne aloft above Alps and Himalayas, where the waters would become part of the everlasting snows and ice, where the ark, in fact, would have become buried in ice for several thousands

of Noah's ark.

of feet, and where, even if such ice-burial could have been somehow overcome, life in the ark would have been impossible apart from some miraculous system of "central heating"![3]

If the flood had been universal, plant life would have suffered irrepairable damage. The water pressure would have been about 800 tons on each square inch of the earth's surface. Trees, grass, and tender herbs would have been greatly reduced or destroyed. In his book *The Christian View of Science and Scripture,* Bernard Ramm says:

> Practically the entire world of plants would have perished under the enormous pressure, the presence of salt water, and a year's soaking. Innumerable life cycles of plants and insects would have been interrupted and would have required a creative work almost as extensive as the original creation to restore the earth.[4]

The Biblical, Theological, and Ecclesiastical Cyclopedia by M'Clintock and Strong has made this statement:

> Experiments as have been made with regard to the action of sea-water upon terrestrial plants leave very little doubt that submergence in sea-water for ten or eleven months would have effectually destroyed not only the great majority of the plants, but their seeds as well. And yet it is not said that Noah took any stock of plants with him into the ark, or that the animals which issued from it had the slightest difficulty in obtaining pasture. There are, then, it must be confessed, very strong grounds for believing that no *universal* deluge ever occurred.[5]

And what about fish? Since fish live in water, we might suppose this would be no problem for a universal flood. But even this is not that simple. When the rains came, the rivers filled and ran into the seas which rose until the entire world was covered — according to the universal flood viewpoint. All water became salty. Some fish can only live in fresh water and some require water of a certain temperature. I don't suppose anyone believes Noah provided climate-controlled aquariums for fish! Quoting again from Ramm:

> The mixing of the waters and the pressure of the waters would have been devastating. Many of the salt water fish and marine life would die in fresh water; and many of the fresh water fish and marine life would die in salt water... Furthermore, the pressure of the water six miles high (to cover the Himalayas) would crush to death the vast bulk of marine life. Ninety percent of marine life is within the first fifty fathoms. The enormous pressure of six miles of water on top of these forms (most of which cannot migrate, or migrate any distance) would have mashed them.[6]

Writing over 100 years ago, Robert Jamieson, in his *Critical and Experimental Commentary,* pointed out some of the problems of a universal flood, including that of animals traveling from remote parts of the world in order to get to the ark:

> We must imagine motley groups of beasts, birds, and reptiles, directing their way from the most distant and opposite quarters to the spot where Noah had prepared his ark — natives of the polar regions and the torrid zones repairing to sojourn in a temperate country, the climate of which was unsuited alike to arctic and equatorial animals. What time must have been consumed! what privations must have been undergone for want of appropriate food! what difficulties must have been encountered! what extremes of climate must have been endured by the natives of Europe, America, Australia, Asia, Africa, and the numerous islands of the sea![7]

Since some animals are found only in one certain land, are we to assume that they came all the way to the ark and then headed back, after the flood, to their native land? The kangaroo provides an interesting example. Russell L. Mixter, an evangelical scientist and Professor of Zoology at Wheaton College, has written:

> Living kangaroos or fossils of kangaroos are found only in Australia. What shall we conclude? If the fossil evidence means

that there never have been kangaroos in Asia, then kangaroos were not in the ark or if they were, they hurried from Australia to meet Noah, and as rapidly returned to their native land. Is it not easier to believe that they were never in the ark, and hence were in an area untouched by the flood?[8]

Kangaroo

After the flood, the divine promise was that such destruction of that land would never occur again. The promise extended not only to Noah and his family, but to the animals as well: "... *from* all that go out of the ark, *to* every beast of the earth" (Genesis 9:8-10). Some recognize a distinction here between those beasts that went "out of the ark" and those described as "every beast of the earth"; that is, animals that were not in the ark. This would only be a theory, but the Biblical wording "from...to" tends to support this distinction. *The Pulpit Commentary* says this could simply be an idiomatic phrase expressing the totality of the animal creation, "though in all probability it was the case, that *there were animals which had never been in the ark.*"[9]

If every single creeping thing on earth today descended from those on the ark, how can we explain the fact that very slow-moving creatures, such as turtles, are found in some of the most

remote parts of the world? Consider again the snail. There are over 80,000 kinds of snails ranging in size from a pinhead to 2 feet, with life-spans ranging from 2 to 20 years.

Picture two snails leaving the ark in the mountains of Ararat. They have survived through the flood, were not stepped on and crushed by elephants and other anxious animals leaving the ark, and have headed in the direction of California. If they could continue to move inch by inch in the same general direction, and all of their descendants did the same, how many thousand years would it take to reach California? When we consider all the detours caused by deep canyons, massive mountains, vast oceans, swift rivers, freezing snow, burning deserts, and many other problems, the journey could not be anything but s-l-o-w!

Top speed for a common garden snail is 0.03 miles per hour, but it only moves occasionally, and in dry seasons it makes no progress at all for it seals itself inside its shell. According to the information and dates given in the Bible, the flood was less than 4,500 years ago. Considering the speed of the snail and the comparatively short time since the flood, how can we explain the fact that there are snails in California?

The three-toed sloth has an average ground speed of 0.068 miles per hour. This is about 6 to 8 feet per minute — only twice as fast as a snail! The three-toed sloth hangs from upper

Three-toed sloth

41

branches of trees by its long, hooked claws and is about 2 feet in length. It is a South American animal. If every sloth was wiped out by a universal flood — except a pair on the ark less than 4,500 years ago — how can we explain the presence of sloths in South America today? Did they leave the ark, travel clear across Asia, miraculously cross the Bering Straits, travel the entire length of North America, Central America, and finally end up in south America — all of this at 0.068 miles per hour?

Though the Bible says that "every" animal in the earth died (Genesis 6:17), we must remember that the word here translated "earth" is *erets*, meaning that every animal in the *land* died. During the plagues upon Egypt, "every" herb of the *erets* was destroyed (Exodus 10:5-15). None take this to mean that every herb in the entire world was destroyed. So, when the same wording is used of the flood — the waters covered the face of the *erets* and destroyed "every" animal of the *erets* (land) — we are not required to believe that all animals in *all* lands died.

If China was not the land designated by *erets,* the giant panda (which is found only there in the bamboo forests between 6,000 and 14,000 feet) was not threatened by the flood. If Australia was not the land designated by *erets,* there were no koalas or kangaroos on the ark. If Central Africa was not the land designated by *erets,* giraffes and elephants were not

Koala

involved. If South America was not the land designated by *erets*, the three-toed sloth survived without making the journey to the ark and back.

A regional flood would involve only animals that needed to be saved from extinction in one area. The wisdom of God would indicate that not more animals were taken on the ark than eight people could properly manage and care for. We believe the ark was an orderly operation, not a gigantic house of horror filled with constant chaos caused by caring for an almost innumerable number of monstrous beasts and reptiles.

4

THE ARK,
ITS SIZE AND PURPOSE

Did Noah invite other people—those outside his own family—to come aboard the ark and escape the flood? Do we know for certain how big the ark actually was? Did it take 120 years to build? Had it ever rained before the time of the flood? If the flood was regional, were there people in other parts of the world who escaped the flood?

The Bible gives the dimensions of the ark as 300 cubits long, 50 cubits wide, and 30 cubits high (Genesis 6:15). It was proportionally ideal—six times as long as it was wide. But just what these dimensions were in feet depends on how many inches we figure to a cubit. If we figure a cubit at 18 inches, this works out to the ark being 450 feet long, 75 feet wide, and 45 feet high. These are very large dimensions, yet even with these, the doorway would probably not have been over 13 feet high. Dividing the height of the ark by 3 (for the three levels) would allow a maximum of 15 feet per level. But we must remember that to support the tremendous weight that would be carried, large beams in floors and ceilings would be required, making actual clearance about 13 feet. The door would have been no higher than this. If huge animals such as African elephants and giraffes were involved—as the world-wide flood would require—some would have had problems even getting in the door! Compare the old drawing "Samantha at the World's Fair."

Samantha at the World's Fair

Those who favor the local flood viewpoint (and, consequently, less animals and smaller animals) do not require an ark this large. Some feel a "cubit" at the period covered by Genesis may have been smaller than what came to be known as a cubit in later times. If so, the over-all size of the ark would have been smaller. There can be little doubt that the way measurements were figured varied in different centuries and from country to country. *Harper's Bible Dictionary* says:

> Metrology (the science of measurement of mass, length, and time) presents a confused picture in Palestine...and the peripheral countries...Not even well-grounded Babylonian metrology adhered to the same standard throughout its history. In the matter of weights and measures, the Hebrew people were influenced by Babylonian, Egyptian, Canaanite-Phoenician, and Graeco-Roman systems...With the coming of each new conqueror, and with every fresh trend in trade, weights and measures continued to *vary*."[1]

In the book of Esther, written under Persian rule, the word cubits may have had a different meaning than in other books of the Bible. The gallows upon which Haman was hanged was 50 cubits (Esther 5:14; 7:9). If we figure these cubits at 18 inches, this gallows was 75 feet high. This seems extremely high for a gallows which stood *in* the house of Haman. If a shorter cubit was in use, the over-all height of the gallows would be much less.

Let it be clearly stated that we are now dealing with *theory,* for we don't know exactly how long a cubit may have been in *Genesis*—the only references being those in connection with the ark and the flood. But suppose the ceilings in the ark were the same as in a standard house today—8 feet high. If the ark was intended to save animals from a local flood only, ceilings of this height would have been adequate. (Only when we start dealing with huge elephants and giraffes are higher ceilings required.) If each level of the ark had an 8 foot ceiling, the over-all height of the ark would have been about 28 feet (allowing for supporting beams for the floors and top). Since the ark was 30 cubits high, this would make a cubit 11.2 inches in length. Figured this way—and this is obviously only speculation—the ark would have been 280 feet long, 47 feet wide, and 28 feet high.

If the ark was 280 feet long, it would have been a very large boat for the time, yet not impossibly so. But if it was 450 feet long, it is difficult to visualize just how it would have been built. Certainly there were no beams 450 feet long. The tallest tree in the world, a California Coast Redwood, is 366.2 feet. The General Sherman Tree in Sequoia National Park, the world's largest living thing, is 272.4 feet. Most trees do not grow over 200 feet high. Just how lumber taken from the short trees of Mesopotamia would be spliced together to support the weight of thousands of tons of animals and supplies through a year long flood is a good question. In modern times, the largest *wooden* ship built was the *Rochambeau* in 1872. It was 377 feet.

To give a comparison, the Great Pyramid in Egypt stands 449 feet 6 inches high. If the ark was 450 feet long, turned on end it would be slightly taller than the pyramid. This would be equivalent to a 50 story building! We do not know what the exact size of the ark was. It is no time to argue over points that cannot

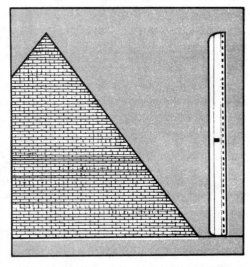

Egypt's Great Pyramid and Ark, if 450 feet, compared.

be proved one way or the other. The world-wide flood concept requires an extremely large ark; the local flood view can live with an ark of smaller dimensions if need be.

120 YEARS?

The idea that the ark was impossibly huge has helped perpetuate a common misconception: that it took Noah 120 years to build the ark. The Bible does not say this. A period of 120 years is mentioned in Genesis 6:3: "My spirit shall not always strive with man...yet his days shall be a hundred and twenty years." These words implied that judgment was coming, but nothing was said about a flood or building an ark *at this time.*

Building the Ark — J. James Tissot

One hundred and twenty years before the flood, Noah would have been 480 years old (for he was 600 at the time of the flood — Genesis 7:11). Noah's sons were not born until he was 500 (Genesis 5:32). It was not until quite some time *after* this that Noah was told to build the ark, for when Noah was told to do so, *his sons had grown up and married.* "Make thee an ark...I do bring a flood of waters ...and thou shalt come into the ark, thou, and thy sons, and thy wife, *and thy sons' wives* with thee" (Genesis 6:14-18). Since it is definitely implied that Noah's sons were grown and married when he was instructed to build the ark, and considering the ages of Noah and his sons, it seems clear that he was not working on the ark for 120 years. A tradition says it took 5 years, but the Bible does not say how many years it took to build the ark.

NO RAIN?

Something else that lacks scriptural support is the idea

that it never rained until the time of the flood. I have heard it preached that Noah looked especially stupid and ridiculous to be building an ark, since it had never rained! The Biblical passage which supposedly supports this idea is Genesis 2:4, 5.

> These are the generations of the heavens and of the earth when they were created, in the day that the Lord God made the earth and the heavens, and every plant of the field before it was in the earth, and every herb of the field before it grew: *for the Lord God had not caused it to rain upon the earth,* and there was not a man to till the ground...

All one can correctly conclude from this passage is there was a time when the Lord had not caused it to rain on the land, a time when there was no man to till the ground, a time when plants had not started growing yet. But soon the plants did grow. Soon a man was formed—as mentioned in verse 7. Though the Bible does not tell us, in so many words, *when* it first began to rain, we believe it is stretching the point to say it did not rain until 1,656 years later—at the time of the flood!

It has sometimes been assumed that Noah, the preacher of righteousness, warned people to escape the flood by coming with him and his family into the ark. But the Bible does not even hint that anyone else was invited—not neighbors, not relatives (such as the parents of his sons' wives), not those who may have helped build the ark—as strange as this sounds. Noah built the ark for "the saving of *his* house" (Hebrews 11:7). If thousands of people were invited to board the ark—and many of them had done so at the last minute—just how there would have been room and food for all of them is difficult to say.

WERE ALL DESTROYED?

When we read that "few, that is, eight souls were saved"

in the ark (1 Peter 3:20), it is easy to assume that eight people were all that survived in the entire world! But, if the flood was indeed a local flood — even though covering a vast area — all this verse would be saying is that there were eight survivors *in the ark*. It may be there were people in other parts of the world to which the flood did not come — people unrelated and separate from the main flow of thought in Genesis.

The reason many Christians have not considered this point is because they feel the Bible says *all* people were destroyed in the flood. *The Genesis Flood,* for example, presents the following statement as a major argument for this belief: "The Lord Jesus Christ clearly stated that *all* men were destroyed by the Flood (Luke 17:26-30)."[2] When we turn to this passage, however, it is far from conclusive that "all" means all people throughout the entire world.

> In the days of Noe...they did eat, they drank, they married wives, they were given in marriage, until the day that Noe entered into the ark, and the flood came, and destroyed them ALL. Likewise also as it was in the days of Lot; they did eat, they drank, they bought, they sold, they planted, they builded; but the same day that Lot went out of Sodom it rained fire and brimstone from heaven, and destroyed them ALL (Luke 17:26-30).

In both examples — the destruction in the days of Noah and the destruction in the days of Lot — "all" were destroyed. In the case of Lot "all" did not mean all people in the world, for it involved only those cities upon which the fire fell. "The Lord rained upon Sodom and upon Gomorrah brimstone and fire...he overthrew those cities, and all the plain, and all the inhabitants of the cities" (Genesis 19:24, 25). This did not include the town of Zoar to which Lot fled (verses 22, 23). It did not include Abraham who witnessed, from a distance, the smoke rising from the plain (verses 27, 28), or cities in other parts of the world.

Since the statement of Jesus about "all" being destroyed in the days of Lot meant only those upon whom the fire fell, it is most natural to believe that "all" destroyed in the days of Noah would mean only those upon whom the flood came. The word "all" is often qualified by the way it is used. If a newspaper article tells of an ocean liner that sinks and all are destroyed, it is understood that "all" means all that were on the ship — not people on other ships, not people not on ships, not people in other parts of the world! So, here, we should be careful not to read into a passage more than was intended.

We saw earlier (p. 15) that the statement about the flood covering "all" the hills meant all the hills in a certain area — not all the mountains or hills in the entire world. It is not straining, then, to suggest that the "all" destroyed by the flood were all within a certain region.

It is true that the New Testament uses the word "world" in statements about the flood — by building the ark, Noah "condemned the *world*" (Heb. 11:7); God "spared not the old *world*" (2 Peter 2:5); and "the *world* that then was, being overflowed with water, perished" (2 Peter 3:6). The Greek word that is translated "world" in these instances is *kosmos,* which is defined by *Strong's Concordance* (2889) as an "arrangement, i.e., decoration, and by implication the world (in a wide or narrow sense)." We believe in the case of Noah's flood, it is best understood in a narrow sense — not the entire world. *Often* the Bible uses a form of speech known as synecdoche, a whole is used for a part, and even words like "all" can be used in a limited sense. When "*all* the world was taxed" (Luke 2:1) or "men out of *every* nation under heaven" assembled on the day of Pentecost (Acts

2:5), it is evident this did not include people from America, Australia, and China.

NOAH A MISSIONARY?

As "a preacher of righteousness" (2 Peter 2:5), no doubt Noah warned of the coming flood. The construction of the ark served as an object lesson for his message *to people who lived in that area.* There is no reason to believe that Noah traveled to lands far away from his own to warn them of the flood. But, had the flood been world-wide, it would seem these should have been warned also! As Ramm points out, "Noah certainly was not a preacher of righteousness to the peoples of Africa, of India, of China, or of America — places where there is evidence for the existence of man many thousands of years before the flood."[3]

Some who recognize that the flood was regional, not universal, still feel it was universal in the sense that all men were drowned. They suppose the entire population of the world was limited at that time to one area. But, as the *International Standard Bible Encyclopedia* says, "An insuperable objection to this theory is that the later discoveries have brought to light remains of prehistoric man from all over the northern hemisphere, showing that long before the time of the Flood he had become widely scattered."[4]

If the American Indian has been in America from around 8,000 to 10,000 B.C., then a universal flood destroying all men would have had to be before that time. But as Ramm says, "there is hardly an evangelical scholar who wishes to put the flood as early as 8,000 B.C. to 10,000 B.C."[5] Again, if the flood destroyed all in the *erets,* land, of Noah — and not all people in all lands — the difficulty is removed.

We might assume from the writings of Josephus, the

noted first century Jewish historian, that he believed the flood destroyed all people in the world. But some of his statements, at least, seem to indicate otherwise. He quoted, for example, the words of Nicolaus of Damascus: "There is a great mountain in Armenia...upon which it is reported that many who fled at the time of the Deluge were saved; and that one who was carried in an ark came on shore upon the top of it; and that the remains of the timber were a great while preserved. This might be the man about whom Moses the legislator of the Jews wrote."[6] Josephus goes on to say:

> Now the sons of Noah were three...these first of all descended from the mountains into the plains, and fixed their habitation there; and persuaded others who were greatly afraid of the lower grounds on account of the flood, and so were very loth to come down from the higher places, to venture to follow their examples. Now the plain in which they first dwelt was called Shinar.[7]

The question is, of course, since there were only eight in the ark, who were these "others" they persuaded to establish dwellings on the plains?

BIBLICAL EVIDENCE

Though it is not spelled out in so many words, certain information within the Bible itself implies there were other survivors beside Noah and his family. The book of Genesis, chapters 4 and 5, mentions *two* family lines that descended from Adam. The line of which Noah was a part is as follows: Adam, Seth, Enosh, Kenan, Mehalelel, Jared, Enoch, Methuselah, Lamech, Noah, and his three sons— Shem, Ham, and Japheth. The other line is: Adam, Enoch, Irad, Mehujael, Methushael, Lamech and his three sons— *Jabal, Jubal, and Tubal-cain.*

The Bible gives a detailed account concerning the

descendants of Noah's three sons after the flood (Genesis 10). But what became of the descendants of the three sons in the *other* line — Jabal, Jubal, and Tubal-cain? Those who believe the flood was universal must conclude that all of these were drowned. But this presents a problem, for the writer of Genesis (who lived long *after* the flood) refers to the descendants of Jabal, Jubal, and Tubal-cain as *still living at the time he wrote!*

> Jabal...was the father of such as dwell in tents, and of such as have cattle. And his brother's name was Jubal: he was the father of all such as handle the harp and organ. And...Tubal-cain, an instructor of every artificer in brass and iron (Genesis 4:20-22).

Notice that the writer says these people "dwell" (not *dwelled*) in tents, they "have" (not *had*) cattle, they "handle" (not *handled*) the harp. Had they been drowned in the flood, this wording would be incorrect. As *The Interpreter's Bible* says, they were "nomads, muscians, and metal workers *existing at the time of writing* [of Genesis]."[8] Hasting's *Encyclopedia of Religion and Ethics* says this wording implies "an *unbroken* history of civilization" and that the writer of this section did not, obviously, regard the flood as "a universal Deluge."[9]

If these descendants of Cain (who had migrated east from Eden) had by the time of the flood populated a different area from that of Noah, and if the flood was regional — not universal — then we have a good explanation of how these people were still living at the time Genesis was written. It is an interesting point.

After the flood, the descendants of Shem, Ham, and Japheth migrated and settled in various countries. "By these were the isles [coastlands] of the Gentiles *divided* in their lands; every one after their tongue, after their families, in their nations... These are the families of the sons of Noah, after their generations in their nations: and by these were the nations *divided* in the earth after the flood" (Genesis 10:5, 32). It is all spelled out in Genesis 10.

But if the flood had drowned all but eight people, how can we explain the existence of these nations to which Noah's descendants migrated and which were "divided" by them? The word that is here translated "divided" (*Strong's Concordance,* 6504) is translated "dispersed" in Esther 3:8: "...there is a certain people scattered abroad and *dispersed* among the people in all the provinces of thy kingdom." If we understand this same meaning in connection with Noah's descendants, they were dispersed among various Gentile nations, implying, it would seem, there were other nations of people who did not descend from those in the ark.

The belief that all nations of the world descended from Noah's three sons is loaded with difficulties. Ramm has made this statement:

> It is pious fiction to believe that Noah had a black son, a brown son, and a white son. The derivation of the Negro from Ham is indefensible linguistically and anthropologically. The justification of slavery from Genesis 9:25-27 is one of the unhappiest examples of improper exegesis in the history of interpretation.[10]

POPULATION CENTERS

If the flood reduced the entire world population down to eight people, so that every single person descended from Noah's three sons, there are difficulties explaining the existence of large population centers within the short space of three generations. Noah's son Ham became the father of Cush. "And Cush begat Nimrod; he began to be a mighty one ...and the beginning of his *kingdom* was Babel, and Erech, and Accad, and Calneh, in the land of

Shinar. *He went out into Assyria* and builded Nineveh, and the city Rehoboth, and Calah: the same is a great city"* (Genesis 10:8-12).

If the flood reduced the world population to only eight people, how — in the comparatively brief time indicated — could there be enough population for Ham's grandson Nimrod to organize cities and civilizations as described?

A period of a few more generations after the flood brings us to the time of Abraham. The Biblical account of his travels reveals the existence of developed civilizations and cities on a vast scale. Leaving the civilization around Ur, Abraham found Canaan populated with Kenites, Kenizzites, Kadmonites, Hittites, Perizzites, Rephaims, Amorites, Canaanites, Girgashites, and Jebusites (Genesis 15:19-21). Twenty-six cities in Canaan alone are mentioned in Genesis at this time. In Egypt he found what was already, by this time, an ancient civilization under the control of a Pharaoh (Genesis 12:15). Near Damascus he rescued Lot and others who had been captured by certain kings (Genesis 14:1-16).

How many years was this after the flood? This is carefully spelled out in detail in Genesis 11. Two years after the flood, Shem became the father of Arphaxad, who at age 35 became the father of Salah, who at 30 became the father of Eber, who at 34 became the father of Peleg, who at 30 became the father of Reu, who at 32 became the father of Serug, who at 30 became the father of Nahor, who at 29 became the father of Terah, who was the father of Abraham (Genesis 11:10-26). Adding these numbers together — 2, 35, 30, 34, 30, 32, 30, 29 — gives a total of 222 years from the flood to the birth of Terah, Abraham's father. Some differences exist on how to figure the age of Terah when

*On verse 11 we have followed the preferred marginal rendering. Micah 5:6 calls Assyria the land of Nimrod.

Abraham was born, but for our present purpose it is enough to say that the period from the flood until the time of Abraham was easily within four centuries. *If* the flood had reduced the entire population of the world to eight people, it is generally acknowledged that this would not allow sufficient time for these civilizations to have developed on the scale described at the time of Abraham.

DATE OF FLOOD

How, then, do those who believe the flood was universal deal with this? They tend to place the flood at a *much earlier date.* The writers of *The Genesis Flood* suggest there may be "gaps of an undetermined length in the patriarchal genealogy of Genesis 11"! Though they feel it is "very hazardous to assume a period of 100,000 years between the Flood and Abraham," they believe "the Flood occurred several millenia before Abraham."[11]

But if gaps of undetermined length can be arbitrarily placed in the genealogy of Genesis 11 — which so carefully and specifically spells out the names and ages of the people concerned — then this information has no real meaning or purpose. There are often difficulties in figuring Biblical chronology, admittedly; but to take what is spelled out as being a few *hundred* years and make it *thousands* of years hardly seems justified.

The regional flood viewpoint, on the other hand, can leave the years from the flood to Abraham exactly as they are — without gaps or guesses — allowing that only part of the world's population was destroyed. This provides a satisfactory explanation for the existence of developed civilizations only a few generations after the flood at the time of Abraham.

The Christian View of Science and Scripture sums it all up in these words:

> The flood was local to the Mesopotamian valley. The animals that came, prompted by divine instinct, were the animals of that region; they were preserved for the good of man after the flood. Man was destroyed within the boundaries of the flood; the record is mute about man in America or Africa or China. The types of vegetation destroyed, quickly grew again over the wasted area, and other animals migrated back into the area, so that after a period of time the damaging effects of the flood were obliterated."[12]

The area of the flood — the land which came to be known as Mesopotamia (now mainly within the country known as Iraq) — is a flat and featureless plain of roughly 45,000 square miles, the largest lowland of the Middle East.[13] "Although scientists discount the possibility that there could have been a flood affecting the entire world at the same time," says *Collier's Encyclopedia,* "there is no question that a vast inundation did take place in the plains of Iraq and the Persian Gulf."[14] *Harper's Bible Dictionary* agrees: "Both literary and archaeological evidence join with the only geographical testimony in the Genesis narrative (Genesis 8:4) in localizing the catastrophe in the Tigris-Euphrates Valley."[15] An old, recognized work on Biblical information also concludes that the flood "extended over the whole valley of the Euphrates, and eastward as far as the range of mountains running down to the Persian Gulf, or further. As the inundation is said to have been caused by the breaking up of the fountains of the great deep, as well as by the rain, some great and sudden subsidence of the land may have taken place, accompanied by an inrush of the waters of the Persian Gulf."[16]

With the fountains of the deep being broken up, some sort of geological phenomenon could have caused an upheaval of land which served as a dam, temporarily, so that the water of the Tigris and Euphrates rivers—along with the tremendous amounts of rain that fell—could have flooded this whole plain. Or, the Lord, who bindeth "floods from overflowing" (Job 28:11), could have made the waters themselves at some point stand "upright as an heap" (cf. Exodus 15:8) to accomplish the same purpose. We don't know exactly, and it is no time to be dogmatic; but any of these possibilities that would limit the flood to this one part of the world seem more feasible than a flood covering every mountain in the world.

IN SEARCH OF NOAH'S ARK

From time to time rumors surface to the effect that Noah's ark has been found on Mount Ararat, having been preserved for thousands of years in ice. Such claims tend to support the idea of a world-wide flood, for otherwise the ark would not be on a mountain that is nearly 17,000 feet in elevation! I believe it can be shown, however, that the ark did not come to rest on what is today called "Mount Ararat," that it came to rest at an elevation far below that at which it would be frozen in ice, and that the stories about the ark being found are unreliable.

I can recall reading one such story in tract form back in 1956. I was high school age and thoroughly amazed at such a wonderful discovery. I was unaware that it did not truly fit with the Biblical information, contained more fiction than fact, and was even inconsistent with itself, as we shall see. But first, we will give this story that has been widely circulated for many years and continues, even today, to be circulated by some.

It is in the days just before the Russian revolution that this story begins. A group of us Russian aviators were stationed at a lonely temporary air outpost situated about 25 miles northwest of Mount Ararat. The day was dry and terribly hot, as August days so often are in this semi-desert land. Even the lizards were flattened out under the shady side of rocks and twigs. Their mouths were open and their tongues lashed out as if each panting breath would be their last. Only occasionally would a tiny wisp of air rattle the parched vegetation and stir up a chocking cloudlet of dust. Far up on the side of the mountain we could see a thunder shower, whilst still farther up we could discern the white snow-cap of Mount Ararat which has snow all the year round because of its great height. How we longed for some of that snow!

Then the miracle happened. The captain walked in and announced that plane number 7 had its new supercharger installed and was now ready for high altitude tests. He then ordered my buddy and me to make the test. At last we could make our escape from the heat, so we lost no time in getting on our parachutes, strapping on our oxygen cans, and in doing the half-dozen other things needful before going up. We then climbed into the cockpits, and with our safety belts fastened, a mechanic gave the prop a flick and yelled, "Contact." In less time than it takes to tell it, we were in the air! No need to warm an engine when *the sun had already made it almost red hot.*

We circled the field several times until we hit the 14,000 foot mark and then stopped climbing for a few minutes to get used to the altitude. I then gazed upon that beautiful snow-capped peak just a little above us and, for some reason I can't explain, turned and headed the plane straight towards it. My buddy turned round and looked at me with question marks in his eyes, but *there was no time to ask questions. After all, 25 miles doesn't mean much at a hundred miles an hour!*

We transversed a couple of miles around the snow-capped dome and then took a long swift glide down the south side and suddenly came upon a perfect gem of a lake, blue as a sapphire, but frozen over on the shady side. Whilst we were circling around, suddenly my companion yelled and excitedly pointed to the overflow end of the lake. I looked and nearly fainted. A submarine? No it wasn't, for *it had stubby masts and the top was rounded over with only a flat catwalk five feet across down the length of it...*

We flew as close as safety permitted, and took several circles around it. We were surprised at the immense size of the thing, for it was *as long as a city block* and compared very favorably to the liners of today. It was grounded on the shore of the lake, with one-fourth of the rear end under water. It was partly dismantled on one side near the front and on the other side was a great doorway *nearly twenty feet square,* with the door gone. This seemed quite out of proportion to modern ships which seldom have doors even half that size.

After seeing all we could from the air, we broke all speed records back to the airport. When we related our find, the laughter was loud and long. Some accused us of getting drunk on too much oxygen. The captain, however, was serious. He asked several questions and said: "Take me up there, I want to look at it!" We made the trip without incident and returned to the airport. "What do you make of it?" I asked as we climbed out of the plane. "Astounding!" he replied. "Do you know what that ship is?" "No!" I returned. "Ever hear of Noah's ark?" "Yes sir; but I don't understand what that has to do with that strange thing 14,000 feet up on a mountain top." "That strange craft," explained the captain, "is Noah's ark. It has been sitting there for nearly 5,000 years. Being frozen up for nine or ten months of the year, it couldn't rot, and has been in cold storage all this time. You have made the most amazing discovery of the age!"

When the captain sent a report to the Russian government, it caused considerable interest and the Czar sent out two companies of special soldiers to climb the mountain. One group of fifty men attacked one side, whilst a hundred men attacked the other. *Two weeks* of hard work were required to chop out a trail along the cliffs of the lower part of the mountain, *and it was nearly a month before the ark was reached.* Complete measurements were taken, plans were drawn of it and many photographs obtained, which were all sent to the Czar. The ark was found to contain hundreds of small rooms, whilst others were large with high ceilings. The unusually large rooms had a fence of great timbers as though designed to hold beasts *ten times the size of elephants.* Other rooms were lined with tiers of cages, somewhat like one sees today at a poultry show: only instead of chicken wire they had rows of tiny iron bars along the front.

Everything was heavily painted with a wax-like material resembling shellac, whilst the workmanship showed all the signs of a high type of civilization. The wood used throughout was *oleander,* which belongs to the cypress family and never rots.

This, together with the intense cold, accounted for its perfect preservation. The expedition also found on a peak of the mountain above the ark, the burned remains of the wood observed to be missing from the ark. Evidently those timbers were hauled up and used to build a shrine, for inside was a rough stone altar, such as the Hebrews used for sacrifices. That timber had either been struck by lightning, or it had caught alight through a fire from the altar. The timbers were considerably charred and the roof burned entirely away.

A few days after the report had been sent to the Czar, that government was overthrown by the Bolsheviks. Our records were probably destroyed by a set of men who sought to discredit religion and all belief in the Bible. Meanwhile, we white Russians of the air fleet escaped through Armenia. Four of us eventually reached America, where we could be free to live according to the Good Old Book, which we had seen for ourselves to be absolutely true, even to so fantastic sounding a thing as a world flood! – Vladimar Roskovitsky.

Just when this story was first circulated is difficult to say. We do know it was carried in many Christian magazines and church bulletins in 1941, 1942, and later. According to one source, it was printed as early as 1 April 1933 by the *Kolnische Illustrierte Zeitung,* announcing the discovery of Noah's ark – as an April Fool's Day joke![1]

Apparently the writer of the story heard that a Russian pilot during the First World War flew over Mount Ararat and saw what appeared to be a boatlike structure, after which an investigation was made. He heard this rumor from the relatives of two soldiers who were now dead, but who had heard the story told by the pilot. From this sketchy and indirect information, the writer enlarged and "wildly exaggerated" the story, as the *People's Almanac* says,[2] putting it all together "in story form with the intent of making it more interesting to read"![3] The story was actually 95 percent fiction and a public apology was given on October 17, 1945.

If one takes a closer look at the story, it is actually inconsistent with itself in a number of places. At the outset the writer seeks to stress how hot it was — a point which helps the story later explain why the ice had melted away from the ark! He tells us it was August, the setting was a semi-desert land, and even the lizards were about to die from the heat! But when he says it was so hot there was no need to warm the airplane's engine because "the sun had made it almost *red hot*," I think he goes too far.

The time for the story was just before the Russian revolution and the fall of the Czar, which would place it no later than the year 1916. By this time airplanes had just barely attained speeds of 100 miles an hour. The writer adds some sensation to the story by mentioning this as the pilot aims his plane toward Mount Ararat: "There was no time to ask questions. After all, 25 miles doesn't mean much at a hundred miles an hour!" But at 100 miles an hour, it would take 15 minutes to reach a point 25 miles away. It seems this would be long enough to ask a *lot* of questions!

If the ark was 45 feet high (as usually figured) and each ceiling of its three levels the same height, no ceiling in the ark would have been more than 15 feet high. If, as the story says, the door was 20 feet by 20 feet, one wonders what purpose a door *higher than the ceiling* could serve. It also seems questionable that the ark would be "as long as a city block," have "stubby masts," a rounded top complete with a five-foot catwalk its full length, and some rooms designed to hold beasts "*ten times* the size of elephants."

The story loses credibility when it says the ark was constructed from *oleander*. This shrub, found in mild climates, grows to 6 feet and possibly as high as 25 feet. I have oleanders growing in my yard. Oleanders most definitely could not provide "timbers" to build an ark!

In the story, the man who saw the ark from an airplane,

apparently had no difficulty flying right back to the spot and showing his captain. If it were really this simple — to fly over Mount Ararat and see the ark — tours to Turkey would quickly swell into a multi-million dollar business! Travel agencies in many parts of the world would be swamped with calls to make reservations! If any suppose the Turkish government would oppose this (the Turkish population being almost entirely Muslim), because it would "prove the Bible true," we can only say this is not valid reasoning. The sacred book of the Muslims, the Koran, *also* mentions Noah and the ark!

Though it took the soldiers, in the story, several weeks to chop out the trail and get there, they too went right to the location. If the actual site were this easily found, one wonders why all the expeditions before and since that time have been unable to find it.

Probably the first person to ever climb Mount Ararat was J. J. Friedrich Parrot in 1829. In 1845 O.W.H. Abich, a geologist, climbed the mountain and erected a seven foot oak cross. In 1850 Colonel Khodzko with 60 Russian soldiers conducted an expedition up the mountain. An English party of five, led by Major Robert Stuart, ascended the mountain around 1856 and saw the oak cross that had been erected by Abich. In 1876 James Bryce, famous author and professor of law at Oxford University, climbed Ararat. In 1888 E. de Markoff, a Russian geographer, climbed the mountain and found a stick on which two previous Russian explorers had carved their initials. He concluded it was probably from the cross Abich had left. In 1893 Henry Lynch, a British merchant ascended Ararat. As he stood on the summit, he was confident this was the spot on which the ark landed, but — as with all the others — found no evidence. He did find a metal plate, inscribed in Russian, that had been affixed to the rocks by Markoff's expedition.

Those who search for the ark, sometimes called "arke-ologists," continue to climb the mountain. Each summer, to quote Gaskill, the hotel at the nearby town of Doguba-yazit "swarms with Ararat climbers or would-be climbers."[4] Large sums of money have been raised for searches. The mountain has been searched by helicopter as early as 1952. It has been photographed by earth-orbiting satellites.

Floyd R. Bailey has given a detailed account of the various efforts that have been made.[5] He tells about John Libi who thought the ark's location had been revealed to him in a dream and who repeatedly searched Mount Ararat in vain, making his seventh and final climb in 1969 at age 73. Another man who convinced people he had seen the ark was, apparently, a mental patient.

In 1948 a Kurdish farmer by the name of Resit was reported to have discovered the ark about two-thirds of the way up the mountain with a portion of it about the size of a house projecting from beneath the ice. Resit's fellow villagers, upon hearing his account, climbed to the site and agreed that it was unmistakably a boat. The account of this, which was apparently carried by the Asso-ciated Press, motivated A. J. Smith, the dean of a small Bible college in North Carolina, to journey to the mountain in 1949. His intention was to locate Resit, hire him as a guide, and verify that the ark had at last been discovered. Unfortunately, however, Resit could not be found. A reward was offered for information. A search of villages "for 100 miles around" not only failed to produce one person who had seen the ark, no one could be found who had *even heard the story!* Still, books written even 30 years later, refer to the Resit story as evidence that the ark is still on Mount Ararat, and conveniently fail to include the disappointing trip made by Smith!

By using bits and pieces of information, piecing together

similarities of stories (and ignoring the contradictions), a movie has been made which leaves the impression that the ark is still on Mount Ararat. One claim that has been commonly made in recent years is that pieces of wood — supposedly portions of the ark — have been found on the mountain. Upon investigation, however, a number of independent carbon dating tests made in various parts of the world, confirm that the wood is only hundreds of years old, not thousands.[6] One by one stories about finding the ark on Mount Ararat have been investigated — some to be exposed as out-and-out hoaxes and others, at best, unverifiable.

In view of all that has gone on, it is almost shocking to turn back to the Bible itself and discover that it does not say the ark rested on Mount Ararat at all! What the Bible actually says is this: "And the ark rested... upon the *mountains of Ararat*" (Genesis 8:4). "Ararat" was the name of a *country*. It was called the "kingdom of Ararat" (Jeremiah 51:27). The word Ararat is but the Hebrew form of the Assyrian Urartu. In the late 7th century B.C., this general area became known as Armenia. After King Sennacherib was assassinated by his two sons, they fled from Nineveh to "Armenia" (2 Kings 19:37). The terms "Ararat" and "Armenia" are both translated from the *same* Hebrew word in the Bible (*Strong's Concordance,* 780), Ararat simply being the older word by which that country was known.

The Biblical expression "mountains of Ararat" shows that during the flood the ark drifted from the flat plains of Mesopotamia into the mountainous country of Ararat. But just exactly where or which mountain is not specified. We see no reason, consequently, to assume the highest mountain in the whole area is intended. The oldest information would place the ark's resting place further south in Ararat among mountains that were lower in elevation and bordering the plain: the Kurdistan mountains.

Clear back in the 3rd century B.C., Berosus spoke of the ark's resting place being on the southern frontier of Armenia (Ararat) in the Kurdistan mountains.[7] Epiphanius simply said the ark rested in "the country of the Kurds."[8] The Syriac Peshitta and the Aramaic Targums of Genesis 8:4 call these mountains where the ark rested the Kardo mountains, as does also the Lamsa version of the Bible. They are named from the Kurdish people who inhabited them. Though the Kurds later migrated further north, according to ancient literary references, they originally lived south of Lake Van in the region that is now northern Iraq across a belt of foothills and mountains that bordered the Mesopotamian plain.

That this area was where the ark came to rest was long believed by the people living in northern Mesopotamia and, with the coming of Christianity, became the prevailing view of the Christian East, including the Syrian church and the Nestorian Christians in northern Iraq.

Early in the 3rd century A.D., Hippolytus in Rome wrote that the ark came to rest "in the mountains called Ararat, which are situated in the direction of the country of the Adiabeni."[9] The Adiabeni lived in Adiabene, the district between the two Zab Rivers, near the north end of the Zagros Mountains. Sextus Julius Africanus, another noted name among church fathers, said that "we know" the mountains of Ararat on which the ark landed are "in Parthia,"[10] which would point us, roughly, in the same direction.

According to the Babylonian version of the flood (which has many parallels within the Biblical account), the ark came to rest on Mount Nisir which ancient records place among the Zagros Mountains northeast of the Mesopotamian plain. The annals of King Ashurnasirpal II (883-859 B.C.) link it with the region south of the Little Zab River.

In Arabic, Nisir is called Judi which is the mountain designated by the Koran: "... and the ark rested on the mountain Al Judi" (Hûd 11:46). A footnote mentions that this mountain is one which divides Armenia on the south from Mesopotamia in the area that was inhabited by the Kurds.

Admittedly, all of these statements do not totally agree with each other, but part of this could be because some areas have been known by different names at different times. The kingdom of Ararat (later called Armenia) had what historians call "elastic borders," varying from one conquest to another, and just where boundaries between the Kurdistan mountains or Zagros mountains may have been,

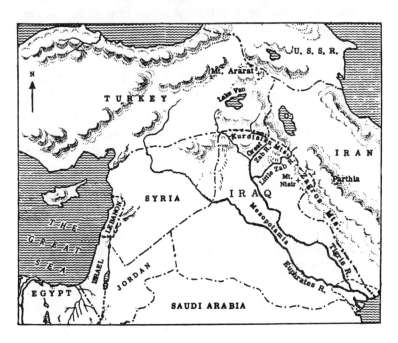

we cannot say. Nevertheless, the bulk of this information would favor a location within the foothills and mountains that bordered the vast Mesopotamian plain in the country that is now known as Iraq, not a location far to the north in Turkey where Mount Ararat is located.

It was not until the fourth century — well over 2,000 years after the flood! — that Mount Ararat (called by the Armenians Mt. Massis and by the Turks Agri-Dagi) was designated as the ark's resting place. If the *age* of a tradition carries any weight, we should bear in mind that this was the last, not the earliest location. It was a natural development actually. Christianity had come to Armenia and with it the Biblical account of Noah's ark. Armenia was the country formerly known as Ararat. Assuming that the flood covered every mountain in the world, the highest mountain in Armenia seemed like the logical place. And, since no one had ever climbed the mountain at that time, no one could disprove that the ark or portions of it were not still up there.

Christianity Today quotes the world renowned archaeologist, Dr. William F. Albright, as saying there is no Biblical basis for the claim that Mount Ararat is where the ark settled. Neither could pieces of wood taken from these heights be pieces of the ark, for the remains of the ark could not be at such a high elevation.[11]

It should be pointed out that the word translated "mountain" in the Bible does not, necessarily, mean a mountain of great height. It is the same word that is translated "hill"! It is, in the Hebrew *har* (*Strong's Concordance*, 2022). It is translated "*hill* of Zion" in one place and "*mount* Zion" in another (Psalms 2:6; Micah 4:7). When we read the words hill and mountain in the flood account, both are from the same word. *Har* simply means an elevated area, something one would go up to or mount, a mountain. The idea that it must mean a mountain many thousands of feet high is simply not true.

At what elevation, then, did the ark come to rest? The Bible does not give us this information—not in so many words—but there are reasons to believe it was not at a high altitude. The oldest information handed down indicates that people after the flood saw the ark and took pieces of wood from it; in other words, it was *accessible.*

Josephus quotes Nicolaus of Damascus who wrote that the remains of the wood of the ark were preserved for "a great while." In another place he states that "remains of that ark, wherein it is related that Noah escaped the deluge ...are still shown to such as are desirous to see them." He quotes Berosus the Chaldean who wrote: "It is said there is still some part of this ship in Armenia... and that some people carry off pieces of the bitumen, which they take away, and use chiefly as amulets for the averting of mischiefs."[12] Statements such as these, of course, could have been based on mere rumor. Nevertheless, they do show that all of these men envisioned the ark as coming to rest at a comparatively low altitude, on a spot that was *accessible* —not on top of a mountain no one (at that time) had ever climbed!

There is no doubt that Mount Ararat is a difficult mountain to climb. Parts of it are steep and rugged. Stories are told of loose pieces of lava rock, some nearly as big as automobiles, and one false step could cause a deathly avalanche. Violent storms come up suddenly on the mountain. The high altitude makes breathing difficult and muscular effort strenuous. These, among other reasons, are given as to why it is difficult to climb the mountain and locate the ark. But doesn't this tell us something? If the ark had come to rest on top of this mountain, how did thousands of animals of all sizes and shapes safely descend from these lofty

71

Climbing over snow and ice—*Ridpath's History of the World.*

heights? Some animals are simply not mountain climbers. Imagine the problems they would have faced as they attempted to climb down over cliffs and across canyons to descend from a pathless mountain! If skilled mountain climbers with all the latest equipment have difficulty climbing up, how did Noah and all the animals climb down?

Mount Ararat is covered by *perpetual* ice and snow from the 14,000 foot level on up. Some of its glaciers are hundreds of feet thick. Those who believe the ark is still "up there" suppose it has been preserved because of the *ice*. But this is the very thing that *disproves* this supposition! If the ark had actually been carried by the flood to this height—to which water freezes because of the extreme cold—it would not have been *floating* in water, it would have been *frozen* in ice! The extreme cold would have made survival for Noah and the animals nearly impossible, even within the ark. Once outside the ark, it is difficult to visualize how all of them could have made the journey down the mountain through miles and miles of snow and ice.

After the ark came to rest, Noah's view of the surrounding territory was somewhat obscured. Perhaps the mountains (or hills) around the ark that were "seen" (Genesis 8:5) were situated in such a way that his vision beyond these was limited. We don't know for certain. We do know that in order for him to determine the flood waters had abated, he sent a dove. Being able to fly high in the air, the dove spotted some olive trees and returned with an olive leaf in her mouth (Genesis 8:11). If, however, the ark had been perched high upon the slope of a 17,000 foot mountain, it seems Noah's view would have been almost unlimited. From there surely he could have determined the level of the flood without the use of a bird.

We know that olive trees thrive best in areas with low

humidity, where summers are long and hot, and winter temperatures do not drop below 10 degrees F. They grow at a low elevation, certainly not on the top of a mountain that is perpetually shrouded in ice and snow. Consequently, had the ark been on top Mount Ararat, the dove would have had to fly *down* thousands and thousands of feet to the level at which olive trees grow and then fly clear back

Artist's concept of dove returning to Noah — J. James Tissot.

74

up with the olive leaf. Somehow, I do not get this picture from the Genesis account.

Look at it this way: Noah had originally sent the dove "to see if the waters were abated from off the face of the ground; but the dove found *no rest* for the sole of her foot, and she returned unto him." *Seven days* later, however, "again he sent forth the dove out of the ark; and the dove came into him in the evening; and lo, in her mouth was an olive leaf plucked off: so Noah knew that the waters were abated from off the earth" (Genesis 8:8-11). If the ark was up high on a mountain nearly 17,000 feet, this would mean the flood level dropped from this elevation, all the way down to the elevation at which the olive trees were growing, in *seven days*. No one believes this!

Finally, from the time the ark rested until the whole flood experience was over is commonly figured at 221 days (Genesis 8:5-14). This is based on a total of all the days and dates mentioned. Some feel these periods may have overlapped and the actual time was not this long. But for our present purpose we will allow that the time was a full 221 days. There is an implication, as we saw earlier, that the water level dropped at an approximate rate of 4 inches a day (page 17). This would be 884 inches for the 221 days. Dividing this by 12 to get the number of feet, we have a figure of 73 feet as the elevation at which the ark came to rest! This could, at best, be only a rough estimate. A lot could depend on the contour of the land, the amount of saturation, whether this would be above sea level or above the level that olive trees grow, or numerous other factors. But in any event, there is nothing — Biblically or logically — to indicate that the ark's resting place was on top of a mountain nearly 17,000 feet in elevation.

There are many difficulties in understanding all the details about Noah's flood. Attempting to face these diffi-

75

culties, the *New Catholic Encyclopedia* has gone so far as to say: "There may never have been such a flood, and the varying descriptions may be the product of man's imagination," suggesting that the whole story might be better understood as a parable![13] We choose to believe, however, there was a Noah, there was an ark, and there was a flood. We can do so, because we believe the regional flood viewpoint provides a workable alternative.

Fausset's *Expository Bible Encyclopedia* says the difficulties that surround a universal flood "make a partial one probable."[14] *The Interpreter's Bible* says a universal flood would be a "physical impossibility."[15] The scholarly and detailed Hasting's *Encyclopedia of Religion and Ethics* says: "The belief in a universal Deluge has long been abandoned by well-informed writers."[16]

I have given what I feel are sufficient reasons to favor the regional or local flood viewpoint. It would be senseless, of course, to make the acceptance or rejection of this position a test of faith or fellowship. I am perfectly willing, as Paul advised, to let every person be fully persuaded in his own mind.

6

JOSHUA'S LONG DAY— How Long Was it?

We have all heard about the time Joshua commanded the sun to stand still and—according to the common belief —the day was extended many additional hours until the battle was won.

Early settlers in the California desert were familiar with the story and are credited for naming the "Joshua tree" which reminded them of Joshua, lifting his hands, and commanding the sun to obey his words.

The story has even been the basis for some pulpit humor.

Joshua tree

A man accused of bootlegging was brought before a judge.

"What is your name?"

"Joshua."

"Are you the Joshua that made the sun stop?"

"No Sir, I'm the Joshua that made the moonshine"!

At the time of Galileo, much attention was focused on

Galileo (1564—1642)

the Biblical account of Joshua. Galileo understood that day and night result from the earth turning on its axis—*not* because the sun travels around the earth. This brought him into conflict with the Romish Inquisition which threatened him with torture and life in prison. Religious leaders at the time, such as Pope Paul V, believed the sun traveled around the earth, the proof being that Joshua's command for the sun to stand still made the day longer!

As well-known as the basic story about Joshua is, however, a serious study of the Biblical account reveals that what *really* happened has been commonly *misunderstood*. The traditional view is that Joshua and his men had fought all through the day until late afternoon. Seeing the sun about to set, and realizing that additional hours of daylight were required to complete the battle, Joshua commanded the sun to stand still, and lo! that day was extended not just for a few extra moments, but for almost a whole day.

Today, however, we all know, as Galileo did, that the length of a day is not determined by the movement of the *sun*. It is the *earth* turning on its axis that makes day and night. Consequently, the passage about Joshua making the sun stand still has puzzled and embarrassed Bible teachers who have tried to uphold the traditional view. In an attempt to harmonize the story with scientific facts, they say it was actually the *earth* that stopped turning, that the only reason the Biblical writer spoke of the sun standing still is because

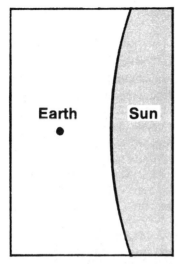 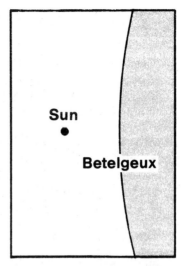

The diagram on the left shows the size of the earth (about 8,000 miles in diameter) compared to the sun (about 865,000 miles in diameter). The diagram on the right compares the sun to the giant star Betelgeux which has a diameter of more than 250 million miles. It is so huge, the entire journey (orbit) of the earth around the sun could fit within its circumference. (See Guinness World Records, *etc.). "The heavens declare the glory of God; and the firmament sheweth his handywork"! (Psalms 19:1).*

he used terms as they were understood *at the time.* It is pointed out that even today we use the terms "sunrise" and "sunset" even though, technically, it is not the sun that is rising or setting. But I believe there is a much better explanation.

Many are surprised when it is pointed out that a hailstorm took place that day. This part of the story, though clearly stated in the text (Joshua 10:11), is not as well-known as the part about Joshua's command to the sun! Somehow the idea of Joshua praying for more daylight does not seem to fit with the sky being darkened by a massive storm!

79

With these thoughts as a preface, we turn to Joshua 10:12-14:

> Then spake Joshua to the Lord in the day when the Lord delivered up the Amorites before the children of Israel, and he said in the sight of Israel, Sun, stand thou still upon Gibeon; and thou, Moon, in the valley of Ajalon. And the sun stood still, and the moon stayed, until the people had avenged themselves upon their enemies. Is not this written in the book of Jasher? So the sun stood still in the midst of heaven, and hasted not to go down about a whole day. And there was no day like that before it or after it, that the Lord hearkened unto the voice of a man: for the Lord fought for Israel.

The expressions used in this text about the sun or moon standing still are translated from two Hebrew words — *daman* and *amad* in the following places: "Sun, stand still [*daman*]...and the sun stood still [*daman*], and the moon stayed [*amad*]... so the sun stood still [*amad*]." The first word used, *daman,* is given in the margin as "be silent." It has the root meaning of "to be dumb" and thus, by implication, "to *stop*" (*Strong's Concordance,* 1826).

The other Hebrew word, *amad,* is defined as "to stand" and is used in various relations literally and figuratively (*Strong's Concordance,* 5975). Within the book of Joshua it is the word used when the waters of Jordan *stood* upon a heap and when the priests, crossing this riverbed with the sacred ark, *stood still.* Though the word is used in a variety of ways, the idea of to stop or quit is evident: the waters of Jordan stopped flowing, the priests stopped marching, etc. Admittedly, both words — *daman* and *amad* — have the meaning of "TO STOP."

But the question is: When Joshua commanded the sun to stop, did he mean for it to stop moving or *stop shining*? We believe he meant for it to STOP SHINING!

The Jerome Biblical Commentary says the Hebrew

meaning, as used in this context, is "stop shining," and refers to the darkening of the sun and moon.[1] *The Biblical, Theological, and Ecclestiastical Cyclopedia* cites various viewpoints regarding this passage, including that which would take these words "to signify merely *cease to shine*."[2] Many years ago an article in *Moody Monthly* presented a comparison of the Hebrew words in our text with parallel usages in ancient astronomical tablets. The conclusion presented in the article is that "stand still" makes good sense if rendered "become dark" — that the sun stopped shining, not that the whole solar system stopped for a day.[3]

What caused the sun to stop shining? This is where the hailstorm comes in! The sun stopped shining on Gibeon because the sky was darkened with storm clouds. In various situations the Biblical writers spoke of "a thick cloud" blotting out the light of the sun (Isaiah 44:22), of turning a day into "darkness" (Job 3:4, 5), of the heavens becoming "black with clouds" (1 Kings 18:45). Ezekiel spoke of God covering "the sun with a cloud," resulting in "darkness upon thy land" (Ezekiel 32:7, 8). Job said, "With clouds he covereth the light; and commandeth it not to shine by the cloud that cometh betwixt" (Job 36:32). During Paul's voyage toward Rome, for many days the sun was not seen because of storm clouds (Acts 27:20).

When Joshua commanded the sun to stop shining, the storm that moved in was of such density that it cut off the sunlight from Gibeon. The attacking Amorites may have considered this a bad omen, providing at least one reason why they fled from Gibeon in terror. As they fled "the Lord cast down great stones from heaven upon them... and they died: they were more which died with hailstones than they whom the children of Israel slew with the sword" (Joshua 10:11).

Why did Joshua want the sun to stop shining upon

Huge hailstones fall on fleeing Amorites—C. Mavrand.

Gibeon? We believe the Biblical evidence indicates this battle took place in the middle of summer and that Joshua was asking for relief from the extreme *heat of the sun* — certainly not for *more* sunlight or an extended day!

HIGH NOON

Contrary to the idea that the sun was about to *set* — and Joshua saw that he needed more hours of daylight to complete the battle — the Bible speaks of the sun as being "in the *midst* of heaven" (Joshua 10:13). "The Hebrew here is not the usual word for midst," says the *Pulpit Commentary*. "It signifies literally, the *half*."[4] The Hebrew word is *chatsi* which is translated over 100 times by the word *half*. The meaning is that the sun was overhead, it was high noon! The *International Standard Bible Encyclopedia* makes this comment:

> The sun to Joshua was associated with Gibeon, and the sun can naturally be associated with a locality in either of two positions: it may be overhead to the observer and considered as being above the place where he is standing or as a locality on the skyline and the sun rising or setting just behind it. But here, it was not the latter two, but at noon, literally in the halving of the heaven; that is to say, overhead. Thus Joshua was at Gibeon when he spoke.[5]

It was at Gibeon that Joshua said: "Sun, stand thou still upon Gibeon; and thou, Moon, in the valley of Ajalon." With the sun overhead — at noon — notice where the *moon* was. The description is quite precise. The moon was "*in* the valley of Ajalon" — not "over," but "in" the valley of Ajalon. Since Ajalon was a low pass, the declining moon above the horizon appeared to be framed in the valley.

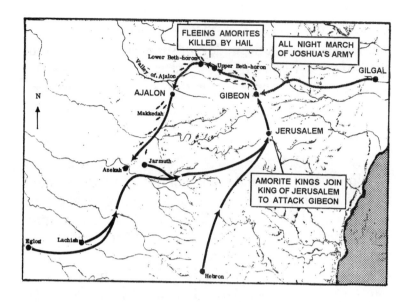

Looking now at the map, the over-all picture begins to come into better focus. Ajalon is *west* of Gibeon. Had the sun been setting and the moon rising — as some have supposed — the moon would have been *east* of Gibeon. This was clearly not the case.

The moon was setting in the valley of Ajalon, *west* of Gibeon. The sun was over Gibeon — in the half of the sky — at *noon*. With the sun and the moon in these positions, it has been determined that the moon was in its "third quarter," about half full, had risen at about 11 PM the previous night and was now within a half hour of setting. The sun had risen at almost exactly 5 AM that morning. It was summertime, Tuesday, July 22![6]

It is not necessary to complicate this paper with the technicalities of how these details are figured (based on the positions of sun and moon, the amount of degrees north of west the valley of Ajalon is from Gibeon, the contour of the land, etc.); nor is it necessary to insist that it was *exactly* Tuesday, July 22. For our present purpose it is sufficient to say it was summertime, it was the month we call July and, consequently, it was *hot!* We believe the reason Joshua wanted the sun to stop shining was to *provide relief from its burning heat.*

Protection from the sun's heat in that land was very important, so much so, that prophets commonly used wording about shade as a type of God's blessings: "A *shadow* from the heat...in a dry place...with the *shadow* of a cloud" (Isaiah 25:4, 5); "The Lord is thy *shade*...the sun shall not smite thee by day" (Psalms 121:5, 6); "... under the *shadow* of the Almighty" (Ps. 91:1); "A *shadow* in the daytime from the heat" (Isaiah 4:6); "The *shadow* of a great rock in a weary land" (Isaiah 32:2).

Jesus spoke of the scorching heat of the sun (Matt. 13:6); "the heat of the day" being the most difficult time to work in the fields (Matt. 20:12); a time when workers "earnestly desired the shadow" from the heat (Job 7:2). "The sun beat upon the head of Jonah, that he fainted, and wished in himself to die," so intense was the heat of the sun (Jonah 4:5, 8).

Relief from the sun's *heat* would help Joshua's men, but a longer day would have put them at a *disadvantage,* as the following details show:

When the Gibeonites sent to Joshua for help it was an emergency message: "*Slack not* thy hand from thy servants; come up to us *quickly,* and save us" (Joshua 10:5, 6). The message was urgent and there was no time for delay. "*So* Joshua ascended from Gilgal, he, and all the people of war with him, and... came unto them *suddenly,* and went up from Gilgal all night" (verses 7-9). This was an uphill march of about 20 miles. Since there had been no advance warning, Joshua's men had no time to rest in preparation for this march. Instead, they had been up all day, marched all that night carrying weapons and supplies with them, and had engaged in a fierce battle until noon. Being summertime, and now the heat of the day — with the temperature possibly as high as 120 degrees — is it likely that Joshua would be asking for more hours of daylight? Would another 12 hours of daylight be to their advantage? Hardly. When Joshua commanded the sun to stop, *there is every reason to believe he wanted it to stop shining!* He didn't want more sunshine, if anything, he wanted *less*!

Professor E. W. Maunder, who was for forty years superintendent of the Solar Department of the Royal Observatory at Greenwich, summed up the situation in these very fine comments:

> From what was it then that Joshua wished the sun to cease: from its moving or from its shining? It is not possible to suppose that, engaged as he was in a desperate battle, he was even so much as thinking of the sun's motion at all. But its shining, its scorching heat, must have been most seriously felt by him. At noon, in high summer, southern Palestine is one of the hottest countries of the world. It is impossible to suppose that Joshua wished the sun to be fixed overhead, where it must have been distressing his men who had already been seventeen hours on foot. A very arduous pursuit lay before them and the enemy must have been fresher than the Israelites. The sun's heat therefore must have been a serious hindrance, and Joshua must have desired it to be tempered. And the Lord hearkened to his voice and gave him this and much more. A great hailstorm swept up from the west, bringing with it a sudden lowering of temperature, and no doubt hiding the sun.[7]

The Wycliffe Bible Commentary, in similar vein, points out that what Joshua deemed necessary for his troops who were already tired from the all-night march, "was relief from the merciless sun... God answered above all that Joshua could ask or think by sending not only the desired shade to refresh His army but also a devastating hailstorm to crush and delay His enemies... The true explanation of this miracle, told in ancient, oriental, poetic style, tends to confirm the idea that Joshua was looking for *relief from the sun*."[8]

NO DAY LIKE THAT

Once a person has been taught the other view — that the day was extended for many additional hours — a verse like Joshua 10:14 tends to support that idea: "There was no day like that *before* it or *after* it." But expressions like this were proverbial; simply a way of stating that what happened was out of the ordinary, unusual. Similar expressions may be found in verses such as Exodus 9:18; 10:14; 1 Kings 3:12; 2 Kings 18:5; 23:22, 25; 2 Chron. 1:12; Ezekiel 5:8, 9; Joel 2:2; etc. What made this day unusual is explained as we continue reading: "There was no day like that before it or after it, *that the Lord hearkened unto the voice of a man*"! We should not read into this verse the idea that the day was unusual because the sun stopped moving and the hours of that day extended. Even if this had been the case, this was clearly not the point here. The point being made, as Maunder says, is that "Joshua had spoken, not in prayer or supplication, but in command, as if all Nature was at his disposal; and the Lord had hearkened and had, as it were, obeyed a human voice: an anticipation of the time when a greater Joshua would command even the winds and the sea, and they would obey him."[9]

After reading that there was no day like this before, and that the Lord hearkened to the voice of a man, we read: "FOR the Lord fought for Israel." What did the Lord do? Comparing scripture with scripture, what the Lord did in fighting for Israel was this: "The Lord cast down great stones from heaven upon them... more died with hail-stones than they whom the children of Israel slew with the sword" (Joshua 10:11).

This explains why that day was unusual and unique. But had the whole solar system stopped moving—this being so much more dynamic—surely the verse would have read: "And there was no day like that before it or after it, *for* the Lord stopped the whole solar system!" But instead, the point of the passage is that the Lord obeyed the voice of a man and fought for Israel. And the way he fought for Israel, specifically, is that he sent a storm which dropped huge hailstones upon the enemy.

A. Lincoln Shute has described the defeat of the Amorites in these words:

> For nearly two miles they ran and stumbled from Upper to Lower Beth-horon. Just before passing Lower Beth-horon, they turned to the south and swept through the wider valley just below Lower Beth-horon to the east, now filled with many olive trees. Just after passing Lower Beth-horon, this valley turns westward along the south side of the hill on which the city stands, and a little farther on it turns southward again towards the valley of Ajalon. Here, out of the mountain passes, they poured into this broad valley, and continued their disorderly retreat southward under the pelting hail till they reached the vicinity of Azekah... Here, apparently, the hail-storm ceased (Joshua 10:11), the clouds broke, and, later in the afternoon, past the heat of that July day, the sun appeared once more.[10]

MIRACLES WORLD-WIDE?

The earth completes one rotation on its axis in 23 hours, 56 minutes, and 4 seconds. This means that the surface of the earth at the equator is traveling over 1,000 miles an hour. If the earth suddenly stopped—causing the sun to *appear* to stand still, as some explain it—the chain reaction of events world-wide would have been tremendous. In 1960 an earthquake in Chile triggered seismic sea waves that caused damage from Alaska to New Zealand and wrecked coastal villages in Japan—a third of the way around the world. If an earthquake could have such far-reaching effects, imagine what would happen if the whole earth suddenly stopped! All human beings, animals, and loose objects would be thrown forward. Oceans would be flung onto land, coastal towns would be devastated, ships at sea would be swallowed by vast waves, and buildings would crumble. There would be literally millions of disasters world-wide! Why would thousands of people living in Italy need to be killed with waves, or the population of Japan terrified with a night twice as long, just so Joshua could defeat a comparatively few Amorites at Gibeon?

Make no mistake about it, God is all-mighty and could provide invisible "seat belts" for all people, hold back the ocean from the coastlines, protect the ships at sea, keep buildings from toppling over and millions of other miracles as he stopped this planet from turning! But why such *complex* and overwhelming measures in order to accomplish one *simple* purpose?

To complicate the whole thing to this extent reminds us of a Rube Goldberg drawing about a machine for washing dishes. When spoiled tomcat (A) discovers he is alone, he lets out a yell which scares mouse (B) into jumping into

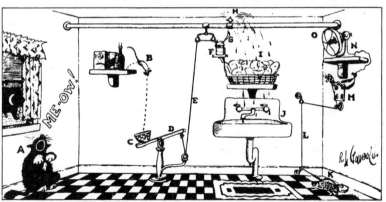

Machine for Washing Dishes — Rube Goldberg. © *King Features.*

basket (C), causing lever end (D) to rise and pull string (E) which snaps automatic cigar-lighter (F). Flame (G) starts fire sprinkler (H). Water runs on dishes (I) and drips into sink (J). Turtle (K), thinking he hears babbling brook babbling, and having no sense of direction, starts wrong way and pulls string (L), which turns on switch (M) that starts electric glow heater (N). Heat ray (O) dries the dishes!

If God suddenly stopped the earth from turning — and performed multiplied millions of protection miracles world-wide — because of Joshua's words, the events that took place at Gibeon would fade into insignificance in comparison! The Bible account of what really happened would be *pitifully incomplete.* We do not believe this is the case.

The New Testament mentions many phenomenal events in Old Testament history — a leper dipping in Jordan for healing, Gideon defeating an army, Lot escaping Sodom, manna falling from heaven, Aaron's staff budding, the exodus from Egypt, crossing the Red Sea on dry ground, the fall of Jericho, etc. But the New Testament never says anything about what would have been a miracle of much greater magnitude: the sun (or earth) standing still. It does not mention the world-wide disasters this would have caused or the miracles that would have been required to prevent such disasters. Does this not seem like a strange omission if indeed Joshua's words set off a chain of complicated and complex events world-wide? How much more feasible — logically and scripturally — to simply recognize that the sun stopped shining and not that it stopped moving!

ORDER OF EVENTS

Taking the information given in Joshua 10, we are able to reconstruct the order of events for this day. Again, the map on page 84 will clarify the locations.

1. Joshua and his men march all night from their camp at Gilgal (verse 9).

2. Arriving at Gibeon, their attack on the Amorites meets with great success (verse 10).

3. The Amorites flee for Azeka and Makkedah (verse 10).

4. Along the road huge hailstones fall on them, killing more than are killed by the sword of Israel (verse 11).

5. *"That day"* Makkedah is taken, smitten with the sword, and camp is set up there (verses 28, 21).

6. The five kings who escaped and hid in a cave at Makkedah are captured, killed, and hung on trees (verses 16, 26).

7. "And it came to pass *at the time of the going down of the sun,* that Joshua commanded, and they took them down off the trees, and cast them into the cave" (verse 27).

There is not the slightest hint from verse 27 that the sun went down almost 12 (or 24) hours later than usual. There is every reason to believe from this wording that "the time of the going down of the sun" was the normal time.

If indeed the sun went down 12 hours later than usual (not to mention 24 hours later, as some suppose!), this would mean that Joshua and his men would have been up the day before their march to Gibeon, marched all night, fought all day until evening, and then continued fighting for another 12 hours during an extended day; that is, a day of 12 hours, a night of 12 hours, fighting all day for 12 hours, *and then 12 hours more* ! This would be a total of 48 hours without sleep. The Amorites, on the other hand, being the ones who planned the attack, had time to rest before and would have been many hours fresher than the Israelites. An extended day would have given *them* an advantage—not the Israelites!

When the sun went down at Makkedah—"at the time of the going down of the sun," the normal time—this was a long enough day without extending it longer!

UNINTERRUPTED TIME

Another point that weighs heavily is the fact that the Bible implies the cycle of day and night has never been interrupted. Clear back in *Genesis* we read: "While the earth remaineth... day and night shall not cease" (Genesis 8:22). Significantly, the word translated "cease" is *shabath,* the word from which sabbath is derived, expressing the idea of intermission, to rest, to cease (*Strong's Concordance,* 7673, 7676). In other words, as long as the earth remained, day and night were not to cease, were not to take a sabbath! But if—at the time of Joshua—night did not come at its normal time, then *the cycle of day and night did indeed take a rest!*

Day and night have never ceased to function right on time. "Thus saith the Lord; If ye can break my covenant of the day, and my covenant of the night, and that there should not be day and night IN THEIR SEASON"—right on time!—"then may also my covenant be broken..." (Jeremiah 33:20). The very integrity of God is linked to an uninterrupted cycle of day and night.

Jeremiah, who spoke these words, lived *after* the time of Joshua. If he had believed the cycle of day and night was interrupted at the time of Joshua, his analogy would not be valid. There is the strong implication that he did not believe the sequence of day and night "in their season" had ever been interrupted.

Those who believe the sun stopped and the day was lengthened 12 or 24 hours, face serious problems of interpretation. Suppose Joshua's command was given on a Tuesday (the third day of the week) — and this day was extended to include what normally would have been Wednesday — then Thursday (the next day, figuring by the *sun* marking off day and night) would be the fourth day of the week, Friday the fifth, Saturday the sixth, and Sunday the seventh day of the week. The whole sequence of days would be off a day from what it had been before! No such thing occurred, in our opinion. The Bible uses the term "DAY" in describing this period — not *days*.

If the time marked by the sun and moon was delayed for 24 hours, then holy days such as the passover would from then on fall on a different day than at the time of Moses. This is unthinkable, for the Israelites were to keep the passover "in the *fourteenth day* of this month, at even, ye shall keep it *in its appointed season*" (Numbers 9:2, 3). If the moon had been delayed for about a complete day, those who kept the passover on the fourteenth day after the new moon, would not be keeping the same 24 hour segment of time as that commanded by Moses! All sabbaths, feast days, and new moon festivals would have fallen within a different 24 hour period than before — each being one day off! This hardly seems to have been the case and so, again, a reason to believe the sun stopped shining — not stopped moving! — at the command of Joshua.

AN EXTENDED DAY?

We have stated that Joshua wanted relief from the heat of the sun — not more hours of sunlight. There is the direct scriptural statement about a storm that moved in which would have caused the sun to stop shining on Gibeon. And there is, of course, the basic fact that stopping the sun would not make an extended day. For these reasons, we have taken the position presented here.

But, coming to verse 13, we read that the sun "hasted

not to go down about a whole day" which, in our English version, does indeed seem to teach that the day was extended. Our translators lived at a time when it was assumed that if the sun stopped it would make the day longer. It is evident they translated the Hebrew words here to fit within that concept. But these words "cannot be *proved* to have this meaning," says the highly esteemed *Pulpit Commentary*. "In fact, it is difficult to fix *any precise meaning on them.*"[11]

Many years ago, A. Lincoln Shute actually visited the area of Gibeon at the specific season when the sun and moon were in the same positions as recorded in Joshua 10— the sun overhead at noon and the moon in the valley of Ajalon to the west. He wrote an article for *Bibliotheca Sacra* in which he stated his belief that the storm caused the sun to stop shining (not moving) and that all the reasonable evidence for this viewpoint "goes far to indicate that [verse 13] probably has some sense that harmonizes with all the rest, *if we only knew all the facts and all of the various shades of meaning in that far away time.*"[12] We agree with this statement and will give several possibilities concerning verse 13.

The Wycliffe Bible Commentary gives the following translation: "For the sun ceased [shining] in the midst of the sky, and [i.e., although] it did not hasten to set about a whole day."[13]

Another possibility is this: We are told that the sun "hasted not to go down." If we are correct that the way the sun stopped was that it stopped shining, then the word "go" would be a reversal of that action; that is, the sun stopped shining and did not hasten to "go" (shine) again until the day was about completed (whole). The word translated "whole" is also translated "full" or "complete" in the Bible. In other words, then, what was said poetically would mean, literally, that Joshua commanded the sun to stop shining at noon, the clouds intervened, and when the day was almost completed, the sun shined again. In the meantime, it "hasted not" — it was not in any hurry, was not pressed — to shine down upon them.

M'Clintock and Strong suggest that verse 13 — the sun "hasted not to go down a whole day" — is equivalent to *withheld its full light*.[14] Again, bear in mind that the word translated "whole" can be correctly translated "full." The word "day" can be Biblically linked with light, as when "God called the light Day" (Genesis 1:5). By omitting "about" (which is not translated from any Hebrew word anyway), the wording "withheld its full light" does present a meaning in harmony with the evidence we have seen.

Another thought: Often when the Bible uses the word "sun," it means more precisely the *light* of the sun, as when we read that the fruits of the earth are "brought forth by the sun" (Deut. 33:14). If it is the light of the sun that is primarily meant in verse 13 — and not the sun itself — it could be said that the *light* of the sun did not go down — did not shine — until the day was almost completed.

This raises the question, however, as to why the expression, "the sun did not GO down" (which sounds more like the setting of the sun itself) would be used. Why would it not be said, if speaking of the light or rays of the sun, "the sun did not COME down"? Realizing that the Hebrew word translated "go" has a wide variety of applications, I wondered if it could just as correctly be translated "come" down. My hunch was easily and quickly confirmed as I checked *Strong's Concordance* (Number 935). Interestingly enough, this word can be translated either way — "go" or "come"! And, in fact, it is translated more times "come" (670 times) than "go" (150 times)!

With this possibility, verse 13 would be saying that the light of the sun (and its excessive heat being implied) did not come down on them until the day was almost complete.

Another shade of meaning may be possible in the word translated "day." The word is common enough, but its specific definition is: "to *be hot;* a day (as the warm hours)" (*Strong's Concordance,* 3117). By applying this precise meaning to verse 13, and realizing that Joshua wanted relief from the heat of the sun, it is possible that "day" could be understood as the *heat* of the day. If so, then "about a whole day" would mean that the sun stopped shining for "about" the whole period when the sun's heat would be oppressive — the hot hours of the day.

Taking this information, then, and including it in brackets, the following gives an over-all view of our text: "Sun, stop [shining] upon Gibeon... and the sun stopped [shining]... until the people had avenged themselves upon their enemies... So the sun in the midst of the sky stopped [shining], and [the light of the sun] hasted not to go [come or shine] down for about a whole [an entire] day [specifically, the hot hours of the day]."

POETIC PASSAGE

Finally, it should be pointed out that the wording about the sun stopping is in a portion of Joshua 10 that is unmistakably poetic in nature. As the *Pulpit Commentary* says: "The poetic form of this passage is clear to everyone who has the smallest acquaintance with the laws of Hebrew poetry" and that these words "belong rather to the domain of poetry than history, and their language is that of hyperbole rather than of *exact narration of facts.*"[15] Poetic passages such as this do not require a literal meaning for each word or expression used.

It was not uncommon for songs or poetic sketches about Israelite victories to be written using non-literal expressions. After the defeat of the Egyptians at the Red Sea: "Then sang Moses...unto the Lord...he hath dashed in pieces the enemy...the earth swallowed them" (Exodus 15). "When Israel went out of Egypt...the sea saw it and fled...the mountains skipped like rams" (Psalm 114). The defeat of Sisera and his armies inspired the poetic portion of Judges 5: "Then sang Deborah... the earth trembled...the mountains melted...the stars in their courses fought against Sisera." When David escaped from Saul, he "spake unto the Lord the words of this song...The earth shook and trembled, there went up a smoke out of his nostrils, and fire out of his mouth ...he did fly upon the wings of the wind...he drew me out of many waters" (Psalm 18).

In all of these examples, the Bible records the actual *historical* account of what happened. These same events are then told *poetically* — stars fighting, mountains skipping, the frightened sea fleeing, the earth trembling, etc. All understand these expressions as figures of speech — all recognize the poetic liberty — even though written about literal, historical battles that occurred.

So it is in Joshua 10. We have a *historical* account of what happened (in verses 1-11 and continuing in verses 16-43) and a *poetic* account (verses 12-15). Each account — the poetic and the historical — ends with the words: "And Joshua returned, and all Israel with him, unto the camp to Gilgal" (verses 15, 43). If we did not distinguish between the historical account and the poetic, these two verses would be in conflict, implying that Joshua returned twice to Gilgal. This cannot be, for the night following the day of Joshua's command, the camp was established at Makkedah (verse 21). We know the historical account continues in verse 16 (from what had led up to the poetic account) because of the words: "But these five kings fled..." What five kings? This must tie back in and continue the historical account from verses 1-11.

Because the wording about Joshua's command to the sun is contained within the poetic portion of Joshua 10, some have understood this simply as a poetic way of saying that "God and all nature fought on the side of Joshua," so that *the work of two days was accomplished in one.* Rabbi Levi ben Gersom, a well-known name in Judaism, put it this way: "The wish of Joshua aims only at this, that one day and night might be long enough for the overthrow of the so numerous forces of the enemy. It was the same as if he had said: Grant, Almighty Father, that before the sun goes down, thy people may take vengeance on this multitude of thy foes. The miracle of the day was, that, at the prayer of a man, God effected so great a defeat in so short a time."[16]

While such conclusions are certainly possible when dealing with poetry, the fact that the historical portion of Joshua 10 mentions a massive hailstorm provides strong reason to believe that the literal sun was involved, its light being stopped by that storm. Yet, being poetic, we are not required to understand each expression or phrase in a strictly literal sense. Bible scholars of all persuasions recognize that when we have a historical account and a poetic account of the same event, we always take the historical account to explain or clarify the poetic — not the other way around. If we apply this rule of interpretation in Joshua 10, a good harmony and sense can be given to this passage which has, otherwise, baffled and embarrassed Bible teachers who have sought to uphold the traditional view.

MISSING TIME?

In 1970, an Indiana newspaper carried a story about scientists in the space program who discovered 24 hours of "missing time." Soon other papers and religious periodicals picked up this thrilling and sensational story. It was printed in tract form. Millions of copies were circulated. But when inquiries were made, the source material could not be located, the part about the scientists could not be verified, and a number of magazines that had carried the story printed retractions. Others felt that any who doubted the story were yielding to Satan! We now reproduce the tract, word for word, as it was circulated and continues to be circulated by some.

"THE MISSING DAY"

I think one of the most interesting things that God has for us today happened recently to our astronauts and space scientists at Greenbelt, Maryland. They were checking the position of the sun, moon, and planets out in space, where they would be 100 years and 1,000 years from now. We have to know this so we don't send a satellite up and have it bump into something later on in its orbits. We have to lay out the orbit in terms of the life of the satellite, and where the planets will be so the whole thing will not bog down.

They ran the computer measurement back and forth over the centuries and it came to a halt. The computer stopped and picked up a red signal, which meant there was something wrong either with the information fed into it or with the results as compared to the standards. They called in the service department to check it out and they said, "It's perfect." The IBM head of operations said, "What's wrong?" "Well, we have found there is a day missing in space in elapsed time." They scratched their heads. There was no answer.

One religious fellow on the team said, "You know, one time I was in Sunday school and they talked about the sun standing still." They didn't believe him, but they didn't have any other answer so they said, "Show us."

So he got a Bible and went back to the book of Joshua where they found the Lord saying to Joshua, "Fear them not, I have delivered them into thy hand; there shall not a man of them stand before thee." Joshua was concerned because he was surrounded by the enemy and if darkness fell, they would overpower them.

So Joshua asked the Lord to make the sun stand still! That's right! "The sun stood still and the moon stayed. . . and hasted not to go down about a whole day."

The space men said, "There is the missing day!" Well, they checked the computers going back into the time it was written and found it was close, but not close enough! The elapsed time that was missing back in Joshua's day was 23 hours and 20 minutes. . . not a whole day. They read the Bible and there it said, "about (approximately) a day." Joshua 10:12, 13.

These little words in the Bible are important. But still they were in trouble because if you cannot account for 40 minutes you'll be in trouble 1,000 years from now. Forty minutes had to be found because it can be multiplied many times over in orbit.

Well, this religious fellow also remembered somewhere in the Bible it said the sun went backwards. The space men told him he was out of his mind. But they got out the Book and read these words: Hezekiah on his death bed was visited by the prophet Isaiah who told him he was not going to die. Hezekiah did not believe him and asked for a sign as proof. Isaiah said, "Do you want the sun to go ahead ten degrees?" Hezekiah said, "It is a light thing for the sun to go down ten degrees; nay, but let the shadow return backward ten degrees." Isaiah spoke to the Lord and the Lord brought the shadow ten degrees backward. 2 Kings 20:1-11.

100

Ten degrees is exactly 40 minutes! Twenty-three hours and twenty minutes in Joshua, plus 40 minutes in 2 Kings, make the missing 24 hours the space travelers had to log in the log book as being the missing day in the universe! Isn't that amazing? Our God is rubbing their noses in His truth! That's right!

There is no need to question the good intentions and sincerity of any who promoted this story. But, as with the Roskovitsky story (p. 63), it is largely fiction. Not only does the story fail to represent what the Bible actually says, it is inconsistent with itself.

First, even if *time* was literally extended almost a whole day for Joshua, it seems more likely this would have been about 12 hours, not 23 hours and 20 minutes. For Joshua's men to continue running and fighting all this time, plus a regular day, after having marched all the night before, seems very improbable. One gets the feeling that 23 hours and 20 minutes are introduced in the story so that when the 40 minutes at the time of Hezekiah are mentioned, it all fits together in a perfect and astounding manner, making the total exactly 24 hours — a missing day!

Having already shown, we feel, that the miracle at the time of Joshua was not one of extended time, but the darkening of the sun by a vast hailstorm, we now turn to the other Biblical reference quoted in the tract about missing time. King Hezekiah had been sick. The prophet Isaiah told him he would not only be healed, but fifteen years would be added to his life. Hezekiah asked for a sign.

And Isaiah said, This sign shalt thou have of the Lord, that the Lord will do the thing that he hath spoken: shall the shadow go forward ten degrees, or go back ten degrees? And Hezekiah answered, It is a light thing for the shadow to go down ten degrees: nay, but let the shadow return backward ten degrees. And Isaiah the prophet cried unto the Lord: and *he brought the shadow ten degrees backward,* by which it had gone down in the dial of Ahaz. (2 Kings 20:9-11).

What has been commonly assumed is that in order for the shadow to move back on the dial, *the Lord had to make the sun go backwards.* I believe this is reading more into the text than is required. Actually all this passage says is that the shadow on the sundial went back ten degrees. The parallel account in Isaiah 38:8 says that "the *sun* returned ten degrees" on the dial, meaning, obviously, the sun*light.* It was not the sun itself that came down out of the sky and rolled around on the king's sundial! It was a miracle of sunlight and shadow *on the dial.*

REFRACTION

Just exactly how God moved the shadow back on the dial is difficult to say. The Bible does not tell us, but I believe the explanation given by Adam Clarke (c.1760-1832), whom no one would accuse of being a "modernist" in any sense of the word, is as good as any. He states that "by using dense clouds or vapors, the rays of light in that place might be refracted from their direct course ten, or any other number of degrees... rather than by disturbing the course of the earth, or any other of the celestial bodies."[1] The following simple experiment demonstrates the effect of refraction:

> Place a vessel on the floor, and put a coin on the bottom, close to that part of the vessel which is *farthest off* from yourself; then move back till you find that the edge of the vessel next to yourself fairly covers the coin, and that it is now entirely out of sight. Stand exactly in that position, and let a person pour water gently into the vessel, and you will soon find the coin to reappear, and to be entirely in sight when the vessel is full, though neither it nor you have changed your positions in the least.

102

Next, Clarke asks and answers a question about refraction:

"Could not God as easily have caused the sun, or rather *earth,* to turn back, as to have produced this extraordinary and miraculous refraction?" I answer, Yes. But it is much more consistent with the wisdom and perfections of God to accomplish an end by *simple* means, than by those that are *complex;* and had it been done in the other way, it would have required a miracle to invert and a miracle to restore; and a strong convulsion on the earth's surface to bring it ten degrees suddenly back, and to take the same suddenly forward. The miracle, according to my supposition, was performed. . . *without suspending or interrupting the laws of the solar system.*[2]

The sun is approximately 93 million miles from the earth. *If* the sun traveled around the earth every day, the circumference of its journey would be about 584 million miles. If in 40 minutes it went back 10 degrees (a circle being 360 degrees), this would mean it had to move backwards sixteen MILLION miles in order to move a shadow a tiny distance on a sundial! This seems quite out of proportion to the actual purpose that was accomplished—a Rube Goldberg arrangement (see drawing on page 89). Of course time is not measured by the sun going around the earth anyway.

On the other hand, it solves nothing to say it was the *earth* (not actually the sun) that stopped and went in reverse. I am reminded of a humorous story that was told back in the '50s when cars with automatic transmissions had become increasingly popular. Not understanding the various gear positions, a man said: "I put it in 'L' for leap, and then in 'D' for drag, but when I put it into 'R' for race, I really got into trouble!" This earth is turning at the rate of over 1,000 miles an hour (at the equator). It does not seem that God Almighty would put the gears of nature into a drastic "R"—*reverse—causing* all kinds of world-wide chaos (or miracles to *prevent* that chaos) simply to show Hezekiah he would be healed of a boil.

A LOCAL SIGN

If the sun moved backward for 40 minutes, *or* the earth reversed itself to give this *appearance* (as some suppose), such would have been observed over a vast area of the world. This was not the case, for certain ambassadors came from Babylon "to inquire of the wonder that was done *in the land*" (2 Chron. 32:31). They had heard, apparently, the news of this wonder and that Hezekiah "had been sick, and was recovered" (Isaiah 39:1). The *International Standard Bible Encyclopedia* says this wonder, being done "in the land" over which Hezekiah ruled, was a *local* miracle, not a world-wide phenomenon.[3]

In the tract, the "religious fellow" told the scientists that "the Bible said the sun went backwards" for ten degrees which caused "40 minutes" of missing time. Of course this is totally inaccurate and the Bible does *not* say this! Even if time was measured by the sun moving forward, if it stopped, and reversed its direction for 40 minutes, and then reversed to continue on, this would be *eighty* minutes!

Suppose I am driving from Riverside to Palm Springs, California. When I get to Banning I remember I forgot something at Riverside. It is 40 miles back to Riverside, but I decide to turn around and return. I pick up what I forgot and continue back on the highway. When I come to Banning again, how many miles have I gone out of the way? I went back 40 miles, so by the time I return to where I had been — round trip — I would have gone 80 miles out of my way. It would be the same with the sun. If it went back for 40 minutes, by the time it again reversed its direction and got back to where it had been, the amount of time "lost" would not be 40 minutes. It would be 80!

Where did anyone ever get the notion of 40 minutes anyway? This is based on the idea of the sun making a circle around the earth every 24 hours. The 1,440 minutes in 24 hours are divided by 360 (the degrees in a circle) so that each degree equals 4 minutes. These 4 minutes are multiplied by 10 (the number of degrees the sun went back), thus 40 minutes.

But this concept is completely erroneous. It was not until the time of Hipparchus (d. 126 B.C.) that the circle was divided into 360 degrees — *centuries* after the time of Hezekiah![4] The sundial sign occurred about 711 B.C. It would be absurd to suppose that Isaiah used a technical and precise scientific term about the degrees of a 360 degree circle when talking to Hezekiah, especially since this concept was totally unknown at the time.

DIAL DESIGN

The whole thing is cleared up once we understand the design of this "dial." According to the Bible, it was actually a series of steps, a staircase, running east and west. As the day progressed, the shadow on the steps indicated how much daytime was left. The accompanying drawing, based on the one given in the *Encyclopedia*

Staircase used for sundial. (1) Progress of shadow in the morning, (2) steps in full sunlight at noon, and (3) advancing shadow in the evening.

Judiaca,[5] shows how this may have been accomplished. In contrast to what we think of as a dial today, with a flat surface, this "dial" could allow the shadow to go back and forth, or up and down, as described in the Bible (2 Kings 20:10; Isaiah 38:8).

The Septuagint version of Isaiah and Josephus say this staircase was a part of the king's house, while a Qumran version specifies these were the steps of the upper story of the house. Whatever may have been the arrangement, there can be no mistake that this dial involved steps, for the very word translated "dial" in our text is *ma'alah,* having the meaning of STEPS (*Strong's Concordance,* 4609). It is the word translated "steps" (1 Kings 10:19, etc.), "stairs" (2 Kings 9:13, etc.), and "degrees"! Notice how *ma'alah* is used in the text: "Shall the shadow go forward ten degrees [*ma'alah* — steps], or go back ten degrees [*ma'alah* — steps] ...And Isaiah the prophet cried unto the Lord: and he brought the shadow ten degrees [*ma'alah* — steps] backward, by which it had gone down in the dial [*ma'alah* — steps]" (2 Kings 20:9-11). It is certain, then, that when the shadow moved back ten *degrees,* it is the same as saying that the shadow moved back ten *steps.* To assume that 10 steps would equal 40 minutes is, of course, *totally unfounded.*

The idea given in the tract — that there were "40 minutes of missing time" — would require us to believe that God moved the sun backward millions of miles. Or, he had to stop, reverse, stop, and start the earth turning again — in order to change the shadow on the sundial! All of this would be unproportional to the actual sign that was given. The magnitude of the miracles that would have been required world-wide — holding oceans in place, keeping buildings from falling over, etc. — would far outshine the sign given to Hezekiah. We would have to ignore the Hebrew word which clearly shows that the "dial" was a *staircase* and that the "degrees" were "steps" on this staircase. And, finally, we would be driven to the absurdity that Isaiah, in speaking of 10 degrees, meant 10 degrees of a circle of 360 degrees, even though that concept was not invented until centuries later!

Since the scriptures imply that the cycle of the earth and sun has never been stopped or interrupted (Jeremiah 33:20), we favor the view that the shadow was moved on the dial for Hezekiah *without involving the motion of the solar system*. If the hands on a modern clock are moved back an hour — as when we switch from daylight saving time to standard time in the fall of the year — we have not changed the *actual* time the sun sets. Likewise, we believe a sign was given to Hezekiah in which the shadow moved on the dial (staircase) without changing the actual position of the sun. It was a miracle of sunlight and shadow, *not time*.

NOTHING TOO HARD

We know there is *nothing* too hard for the Lord (Genesis 18:14; Jeremiah 32:17). Consequently, if a Biblical passage is capable of two different explanations, some are prone to believe that the one that is the *most miraculous* is correct. This is not necessarily true. Roman Catholics are taught that during mass a miracle turns the elements of bread and wine into the actual body and blood of Christ. Are Protestants "unbelievers" because they hold an interpretation that does not require this miraculous change? Would God be any greater if he had taken the Israelites across the Mediterranean Sea instead of the much narrower Red Sea? Would the deity of Christ be greater if he fed 100,000 people instead of 5,000? Would the miracle of his resurrection be more important if he had been in the tomb 300 days instead of 3?

As with numerous great persons in history, legends and stories about Jesus were written in the centuries that followed. Some of these attributed great miracles to him. One second century work, for example, the book of *The Infancy* tells of miracles he performed as an infant. Church leaders rejected this book along with many others for inclusion within the sacred canon, and (we believe) with good reasons. Nevertheless, for a moment, consider the following summary of miracles contained in its first sixteen chapters:

After Jesus was born in Bethlehem, a mid-wife who had been sick, touched the baby Jesus and was healed. When he was circumcised, she put the foreskin in an alabaster box of spikenard and gave it to her son who was a druggist. Eventually he sold the box to the woman who later anointed the feet of Jesus! The mother of Jesus gave the wisemen one of his swaddling clothes which, when they discovered it would not burn, worshipped it. Mary washed the clothes of Jesus and hung them out to dry. When a boy who was demon-possessed touched them, the demons came out of his mouth, flying away in the shape of crows and serpents. A woman who was about to be married, but could not speak because of a sorcerer's curse, was healed when she hugged the baby Jesus.

A girl with leprosy washed with water in which Jesus had been bathed and was healed. Later, along with Joseph and Mary, she met some women who kept a mule in their house which they clothed, kissed, and fed. They said it was their brother who had been turned into a mule by a jealous witch. But when Mary put the baby Jesus on its back, the mule turned again into a handsome young man who later married the girl who had been healed of leprosy!

At age seven, Jesus and other children made oxen, donkeys, and birds out of clay. Each boasted of his work, but the ones Jesus made came to life so that they walked and flew! Joseph "was not very skillful at his carpenter's trade" and in making gates, or milk-pails, or boxes, did not always cut boards the right length. But in taking Jesus along he had no problem, for the young boy would perform miracles, making the boards longer or shorter as needed![6]

Now, are we lacking in spirituality, are we unbelievers, if we reject these miracles? Certainly Jesus, as a boy, could have been used of God to perform miracles, but the Bible itself seems to rule this out. There is the definite implication that it was not until after his anointing with the Holy Spirit at age 30 that his miracle ministry began (Acts 10:38; John 2:11).

The point we would make is simply this: There is no reason to accept one viewpoint as being the correct one simply because it requires more miracles. The following Bible events (several of which I have discussed in more detail in another book[7]) will provide some interesting examples.

MIRACLE CLOTHES?

During the 40 years in the wilderness, the clothing and shoes of the Israelites did not grow old upon them (Deut. 8:4). Does this mean they had miracle clothes that would not wear out? Or does this mean God provided for them so that they did not have to wear old clothes? Adam Clarke has given this explanation: "The plain meaning of this much tortured text appears to me to be this: 'God so amply provided for them all the necessaries of life, that they never were obliged to wear tattered garments, nor were their feet injured for the lack of shoes'."[8] Among them were various kinds of workers, carvers, jewelers, weavers, and there is no reason to believe they did not also have shoe cobblers and tailors. They had the ability, materials, and did in fact make garments, as they did for the high priest (Exodus 28:1-5).

Most who entered the promised land were either under 20 at the beginning of the Exodus or were born during that time. If each person wore the same garment for 40 years, this would mean that thousands of them had garments that *miraculously stretched* as they grew up! Why is this not mentioned, since this would be a *greater* miracle? Would this even be desirable — no change, just the same garment for each person all those years? Their clothes did not wear out upon them; that is, they did not have to wear old clothing. Their shoes did not wear out upon their feet; that is, they did not have to wear worn out shoes. The miracle was in the fact they were supplied with these necessary things — even in the wilderness.

CROSSING JORDAN

When they crossed the Jordan to enter the promised land, the drying up of those waters *may* have been caused by a landslide upstream. We know that such landslides have occurred a number of times — in 1914 the flow was stopped for 24 hours and in 1927 for 21 hours. *The Interpreter's Bible* commentary says: "While not minimizing the fact of divine intervention which the narrative insists upon, it is possible to link the event to natural causes. Frequently in recent history earthquake shocks have collapsed sections of the high clay bluffs beside the river into the narrow stream, effectively daming its flow."[9]

Notice what the Biblical wording says: "The waters which came down from above stood and rose up upon a heap very far from the city Adam, that is beside Zaretan: and those that came down toward the sea of the plain, even the salt sea, failed, and were cut off" (Joshua 3:16). The mention of the city Adam (Adamah) and Zaretan tends to support the belief that a landslide at Adamah caused the waters to back up from that city even unto Zaretan, a distance of 12 miles. There is no need to argue about this point, for whether the invisible power of God stopped the waters at Adamah, causing them to back up for the 12 miles, or whether this was accomplished by a landslide, either way the purpose of God was accomplished so that further downstream his people crossed to the other side!

WATER IN THE DESERT

When "Moses lifted up his hand, and with his rod smote the rock twice: and the water came out abundantly" (Numbers 20:7-11), George M. Lamsa, noted translator of the Bible from Aramaic manuscripts, says the rock he smote was the cover of a *well.* To "smite a rock" in Aramaic does not literally mean to belabor a mass of mineral matter, he points out, but rather to strike a stone which has been placed over the top of a well that has become covered with sand. It is comparable to the English expression "to strike oil," which means, "to find oil."

In that vast desert, wells were considered the property of certain tribes. When migrating, they would cover wells with stones to protect the water supply from sandstorms until their return. If certain landmarks were obliterated, the exact location of a well would be lost. In that case, they would probe in the sand, hoping to "strike the rock." If found, the sand would be scooped away and the well uncovered. So was it with Moses, according to Lamsa. Because of divine guidance, Moses was able to strike the rock and locate the well.

Our first reaction to this interpretation—that the miracle involved a well—might be that of total rejection. *But,* turning to the very next chapter, this interpretation does appear to have support, for the source of the water on this occasion is specifically called a well! "And from thence they went to Beer [a Hebrew word meaning *well*]: that is the *well* whereof the Lord spoke unto Moses, Gather the people together, and I will give them water. Then Israel sang this song, Spring up, O *well;* sing ye unto it: the princes digged the *well,* the nobles of the people digged it, by the direction of the lawgiver, with their staves" (Numbers 21:16-18). If indeed the rock Moses struck was a well cover, buried with sand, we can easily picture the nobles digging away the sand, removing the cover, and allowing the water to flow out.

THE LOST AXEHEAD

When Elisha helped a man who had lost the head of an axe in the water, he "cut down a stick and cast it in thither; and the iron did swim [surface]. Therefore said he, Take it up to thee. And he put out his hand, and took it" (2 Kings 6:5-7). Lamsa says the iron came to the top of the water because Elisha *stuck the stick into the hole of the axehead.* The miracle, as in the case of Moses, was that of divine guidance. When he stuck the stick into the muddy water it went right into the axehead. So, from the Aramaic text, Lamsa translates this verse: "And he cut off a stick and thrust it in there; and it stuck in the hole of the axehead."[10] *If* this is the correct meaning, it would provide a good explanation as to why a stick was used. Had God intended the iron to surface by itself, why was any stick used at all?

ELIJAH AND AHAB

Following the defeat of the prophets of Baal on Mount Carmel, "Ahab rode, and went to Jezreel. And the hand of the Lord was on Elijah; and he girded up his loins, and *ran before Ahab to the entrance of Jezreel*" (1 Kings 18:45, 46). It may be that Elijah was given supernatural strength to run before Ahab's horse or chariot, so that he miraculously arrived at Jezreel before Ahab did. I have heard it preached that he could outrun the finest Olympic champions! But it could be, simply, that he put himself at the head of a company of chanters who ran, as the custom was, before the king reciting his praise or the praises of

God. Other verses mention this custom of men running in front of the king's chariot (1 Samuel 8:11). When Absalom claimed the kingly authority, fifty men were appointed to run in front of his chariot (2 Samuel 15:1).

RAVENS OR ARABIANS?

In the Biblical passage that says "ravens brought [Elijah] bread and flesh" to sustain him (1 Kings 17:2-6), the word translated "ravens" could be translated "Arabians." Did *unclean* birds *steal* food from someone's table and transport it to the prophet? This seems unlikely. There are several strong arguments for the word "Arabians" as the correct translation. But either way, ravens or Arabians, God met the needs of the prophet and this is the main thing!

As one seeks to understand what really happened during Biblical events, there is no need to minimize *or* magnify a miracle beyond what the Bible actually says. For Christians, believing in *miracles* should be no problem. The very incarnation of Christ, his life, his death, his resurrection, and his ascension are all in the miracle-realm. He was in the world and the world was made by him (John 1:10). If he could make this world, certainly *he can do what he wants with it!* This is not the issue.

Certainly God could use ravens to feed a prophet. Certainly God could bring an axehead to the surface of the water without a stick. Certainly God could stretch the clothing of infants to fit their bodies at each stage of growth to adulthood. Certainly God could make the sun go backwards millions of miles to show Hezekiah he would be healed of a boil. Certainly God could stop the whole solar system for a day while Joshua killed Amorites. The question is not, "Can God?" (cf. Psalms 78:19). It is not a question of what God can or cannot do, but what is consistent with scripture. When there is a *simple* explanation, I see no need

113

to insist on the *complex*. When God's purpose of defeating the Amorites for Joshua could be accomplished through a local hailstorm, it hardly seems necessary to stop and start the whole solar system. When simply moving a shadow on a sundial could provide a sign to Hezekiah in Jerusalem, it hardly seems necessary that God would involve every city in the world by stopping, reversing, stopping, and starting the earth turning again!

8

WAS SATAN ONCE AN ANGEL IN HEAVEN?

Many have been taught that Satan was once a beautiful angel who became lifted up with pride, sinned against God, and was cast out of heaven. Does not Ezekiel 28 say he was perfect until iniquity was found in him? And does not Isaiah 14 speak of him as Lucifer, a powerful angel who sought to be as God? Hal Lindsey has echoed these ideas in his book *Satan is Alive and Well on Planet Earth,* stating that Satan was once ...

"the ruler and leader of the angelic beings and apparently led them in their praise of God and shouts of joy... the greatest being God ever created, one who had unequaled strength, wisdom, beauty, privilege, and authority...The blameless, perfect Lucifer was created without any form of evil...with the greatest intelligence of any created being... Lucifer, realizing how beautiful he was, inflated with power and pride, rebelled against God," was cast out of heaven and became the Devil.[1]

Satan?

There was a time when many of us supposed these things were taught in the book of Ezekiel, chapter 28, within the prophecy about the king of Tyrus. But I will say this quite simply:

The *subject* of this prophecy was "a MAN" (verse 2); *not* an angel!

The *location* was Tyrus (Tyre), a very wealthy city; *not* heaven!

The *time* of the prophecy was the 6th century B.C.; *not* something that happened before human history began!

A study of the entire chapter shows this leader of Tyrus had become very proud. Though a mere man, he thought of himself as a god (verse 2). His wisdom and wealth are mentioned (verses 3-5). But none of these things would save him from his destined ruin: "I will bring thee to ashes upon the earth... thou shalt be a terror, and never shalt thou be any more" (verses 18, 19).

HIS WISDOM

"Son of man, take up a lamentation upon the king of Tyrus, and say unto him, Thus saith the Lord God; Thou sealest up the sum, full of wisdom" (verse 12). Elaborate *fiction* has been built on this statement by those who apply this to Satan. They tell us he was the "greatest intelligence," that his wisdom was unequaled, that he had wisdom of the highest heavenly order! But *what kind* of wisdom did he have? It was the *wisdom of knowing how to make money!* "With thy *wisdom*... thou hast gotten thee *riches* ...gold and silver into thy treasures. By thy great *wisdom* and by thy *traffick* [trading, commercial activities] hast thou increased thy *riches*" (verses 4, 5).

Because of pride, God said: "I will bring strangers upon thee, the terrible of the nations: and they shall draw their

116

swords against the beauty of thy wisdom" (verse 7). The "terrible of the nations" were the armies of Nebuchadnezzar, king of Babylon (Ezekiel 30:11). None of this could possibly pertain to an angel in heaven before human history began!

HIS JEWELS

"Every precious stone was thy covering [adornment for clothing], the sardius, topaz, and the diamond, the beryl, the onyx, and the jasper, the sapphire, the emerald, and the carbuncle, and gold" (Ezekiel 28:13). These same stones were also on the garments of the high priest of the Israelites (Exodus 28:15-20). We know that such jewels were available to the king of Tyrus, for he traded with countries which offered "*all* precious stones, and gold" (Ezekiel 27:22). We know, also, that the people of Tyrus were skilled in delicate work, such as the setting of stones. When Solomon wanted a man who had wisdom to do such work in connection with the temple, he sent for a man of *Tyre* (1 Kings 7:13, 14).

The splendor of the king of Tyrus is further described in these words: "The workmanship of thy tabrets and of thy pipes was prepared in thee in the day thou wast created" (verse 13). The word translated "workmanship" here is also found in Exodus and used of one who could do very fine work with jewels (Exodus 31:3, 5). Some feel this verse pictures the pomp of the king, surrounded with girls of the harem who with timbrels danced to his honor.

HIS PERFECT BEAUTY

The king of Tyrus was described as being "perfect in beauty" (verse 12). But this does not imply he was a beautiful angel in heaven, for the same writer also said this about the city of Jerusalem! "And thy renown went forth among the heathen for thy *beauty:* for it was *perfect*" (Ezekiel

16:14). The same was said about the *city* of Tyrus: "... O Tyrus, thou hast said, I am of *perfect* beauty." This statement is followed by a description of the city, its wealth, and commercial abundance. Then in verse 11, referring to its armies, we read: "They hanged their shields upon thy walls roundabout; they have made thy beauty *perfect*."

Of the king of Tyrus it was said: "Thou wast perfect in thy ways from the day that thou wast created, till iniquity was found in thee" (Ezekiel 28:15). Once a person has the idea already in mind that Satan was a beautiful and sinless angel in heaven, this verse seems to fit that idea very well. However, the word translated "perfect" here, *tamiym,* does not imply sinlessness. It is used of men such as Noah and Abraham (Genesis 6:9; 17:1), of sacrificial animals "without blemish" (Ezekiel 43-46), of a vine "when it was whole" (Ezekiel 15:5), and in a variety of ways within the scriptures.

But regardless of this, Ezekiel 28:15 does not say the king of Tyrus was a perfect *being.* It says he was perfect *in his ways*—apparently in his ways as leader, as king! He was "perfect" in his ways *until* this perfection was marred by "iniquity." If we can determine what this iniquity was, we may better understand what is implied by the use of the word perfect. Notice verse 18: "... by the iniquity of thy TRAFFICK"! The word "traffick" (*Strong's Concordance,* 7404) has the meaning of trade, as peddled, and is linked with a word expressing travel in connection with selling. It is exactly the same word translated "merchandise" in verse 16: "By the multitude of thy MERCHANDISE they have filled the midst of thee with violence, and thou hast *sinned.*"

We do not know the whole story, but it is certain that the king of Tyrus was made very rich through trading, through commercialism. But then the wisdom that had gotten him such wealth became corrupted. Thus, what had been a perfect political career, was marred by "iniquity" —

iniquity that was linked with his commercial activities. This
is clear.

A list of the countries and cities with which he traded
is given in Ezekiel 27—places such as Egypt, Tarshish,
Javan, Tubal, Meshech, Dedan, Syria, Judah, Israel,
Damascus, etc. Since the iniquity that marred his perfection
involved trade relations with these countries, we can see
how strained it is to teach this refers to Satan (as a perfect
being in heaven) long before places such as Egypt, Judah,
or Sheba existed!

HIS CREATION

We read in Ezekiel 28 that the king of Tyrus was *created:*
". . . in the day that thou wast created." It is sometimes
argued that man (since Adam) is not created, he is born.
Therefore, even though the king of Tyrus was a man, there
must be a *deeper* meaning—the passage must be talking
about a beautiful angel who was created. But the word
translated "created," *bara,* is simply not strong enough to
support this conclusion. In other references in Ezekiel, it
is used of the Ammonites (Ezekiel 21:30), is translated
"choose" (verse 19), and "dispatch" (Ezekiel 23:47). It is
obviously capable of varied translations and can add no
support to the idea that the king of Tyrus was some special
creation prior to human history.

Besides, the creation of the king of Tyrus probably does
not refer to his beginning as a person, but to his *beginning
as king.* "In the *day* that thou was created" could very easily
refer to the day he was made king. Since the highly deco-
rated royal robes became his covering or clothing in the
day that he was created (verse 13), it seems clear that the
day of his being made king is meant.

THE ANOINTED CHERUB

"Thou art the anointed cherub that covereth" (verse 14). The word translated "anointed" here is not the usual word so translated, but carries the meaning of *outspread*. The cherubims in the tabernacle and Solomon's temple were formed in such a way that their wings spread over the ark, possibly to symbolize protection. Similarly, the king was the protector of the people of Tyrus. The word "covereth" is said to mean one "who leads." Some have taken this to mean that Satan once led the angelic choirs of heaven in their praise of God! This is wild *speculation*. The more natural meaning would be that the king of Tyrus led the people as their king—not that he was merely a song leader!

EDEN THE GARDEN OF GOD

One question remains concerning the king of Tyrus. What about the phrase: "Thou hast been in EDEN the garden of God" (Ezekiel 28:13)? This, more than any other part of the passage, has caused some to believe a deeper meaning is intended. Since it was thousands of years before the time of Ezekiel that the serpent tempted Eve, they feel the meaning of the "king of Tyrus" must be expanded to include Satan.

It should be pointed out, however, that the expression about being in Eden is best understood as IRONY. This is a form of ridicule or sarcasm which means the OPPO-SITE of the literal sense of the words used. When Michal said to David, "How glorious was the king of Israel today!" (2 Samuel 6:20), she clearly did *not* think he was glorious at all. This was irony. When Elijah, mocking the prophets of Baal, said: "Cry aloud: for he is a god..." (1 Kings 18:27), he did *not* mean Baal was a god. It was irony. When Jesus said, "Make to yourselves friends of the mammon of unrighteousness" (Luke 16:9), this was irony, for the context shows this was just the *opposite* of his teaching!

In Ezekiel 28, there are repeated uses of irony. "Thou hast said, I am a god, I sit in the seat of God... Thou art wiser than Daniel; there is no secret that they can hide from thee.... Thou hast been in Eden the garden of God... Thou art the anointed cherub that covereth... thou wast upon the holy mountain of God"! To paraphrase this irony, we might say: "You are really smart. You know everything! You are wiser than Daniel. You were not born yesterday. You know so much, doubtless you were with Adam in Eden. You were upon the holy mountain with Moses. You are even an anointed cherub. You are a god!"

Understood as irony, the actual meaning would be that he was *not* wiser than Daniel. He was *not* in Eden with Adam. He was *not* on the mountain with Moses. He was *not* a cherub or god. That this is the proper sense is evident, for the divine rebuttal says: "Thou art a man, and *not God,* though thou set thine heart as the heart of God" (verse 2).

If, however, some feel the expression about being in Eden requires a more literal interpretation, the point that the king of Tyrus was a man — not an angel — is still not weakened. This becomes apparent once we understand that Eden was a country *at the time of the king of Tyrus!* In fact, it was a country with which he carried on trade!

THE LAND OF EDEN

We must ask a degree of patience on the part of the reader as we take time to point out some things about Eden that have not been commonly understood. Back in the book of Genesis we read that "the Lord God planted a garden eastward *in* EDEN; and there he put the man whom he had formed" (Genesis 2:8). Eden was the name of a *land.*

It was within this land, specifically in the eastern part of that land, that the garden was planted. There is no reason to assume that "Eden" was the name of the garden itself. Technically they are not the same. We could not correctly speak of "California" as though it were synonymous with "Yosemite Park." Yosemite Park is *in* California. The garden was *in* Eden. This is certainly not a major point, but it does provide some scriptural clarification.

To go a step further, when the writer of Genesis refers to this land as Eden, this was probably not the name of this land *when* the garden was planted there. It is doubtful it would have had any name at that point. Eden was probably the name by which this land had become known *at the time Genesis was written*. Since the events recorded in Genesis cover thousands of years—from Adam to Joseph—this would have been long *after* the garden had been planted. The following examples will illustrate this point:

The writer of Genesis mentions a river at the time of Adam that flowed by the "land of HAVILAH" (Genesis 2:11). But that land was not known by this name *at the time,* for Havilah, the man from whom this land took its name, was not born until centuries later. He was a great grandson of Noah (Genesis 10:7).

A place is referred to by the name ZOAR in Genesis 13:10, though it was not actually named this until Lot fled there in Genesis 19:22! Prior to this it was called Bela (Genesis 14:2, 8).

In Genesis 12:8 we read that Abraham journeyed "unto a mountain on the east of BETHEL, and pitched his tent." The writer of Genesis calls this place Bethel, even though it was not known as Bethel *at the time* Abraham was there! It was not called Bethel until many years later when Abraham's grandson, Jacob, named it. "And Jacob...called the name of that place Bethel; but the name of that city was called Luz at the first" (Genesis 28:18, 19).

For a writer to refer to places by the names they are known at the time he is writing is not unusual. An article about New York in the *Americana* says that "Verrazano sailed his ship into New York Bay in April 1524 but left after a brief visit." We all understand, of course, that it was not called New York Bay *at the time*. New York was not there. Even later when a colony was established, it was called New Amsterdam. It was not until the English took it over in 1664 that it came to be called New York!

We might talk about the Pilgrims landing at Plymouth Rock, yet the rock was not known by this name *at the time*. It was called this later because of the colony that was organized and named New Plymouth. We read in Exodus 15:23 that the Israelites "came to Marah" but could not drink the waters because they were bitter, "therefore the name of it was called Marah [bitterness]." Obviously it was not known by this name *when* they arrived there, but as a result of their being there.

The writer of Genesis could have spelled it all out. He might have said: "The Lord planted a garden in the eastern part of the land that is now called Eden." But knowing that the readers — to whom his writings were originally addressed — would understand this, he simply stated that the Lord had planted a garden eastward in Eden, and quite freely refers to it as the garden IN Eden or as the garden OF Eden. None of this would indicate, necessarily, that Eden was the name of that land at the time of Adam.

Just when the word Eden was first used as the name of this land we cannot say with certainty. Obviously it had become known by this name at the time Genesis was compiled. *Harper's Bible Dictionary* links the word "Eden" with *edinu,* meaning "plain."[2] There can be little doubt that Eden was located somewhere on the plain known as Mesopotamia. Two rivers linked with Eden, the Euphrates and the Hiddekel (better known to us as the Tigris, its Greek name) flow through this area. People who lived in Telassar are called "the children of Eden" (Isaiah 37:12; 2 Kings 19:12). Thelasar is the name of a province captured by the Assyrians and mentioned in Assyrian inscriptions as Tilasuri. It extended along both sides of the middle reaches of the Euphrates River. We do not know the exact boundaries of the land of Eden—if there even were such boundaries—but the general area of this land is indicated on the accompanying map.

With this information in mind, we now return to the book of Ezekiel and the statement that the king of Tyrus had been in Eden. Ezekiel 27 lists countries with whom the king of Tyrus did business—places such as Tarshish, Javan,

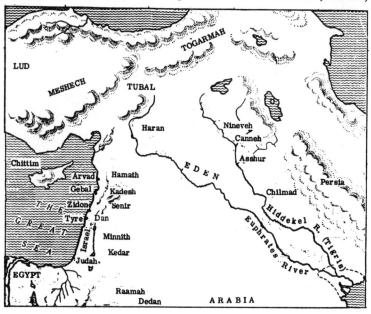

Tubal, Dedan, and Syria; "Judah, and the land of Israel, they were thy merchants: they traded in thy market wheat ...honey...oil and balm." Also included in the list are these: "Haran, and Canneh, and EDEN (!), the merchants of Sheba, Asshur, and Chilmad, were thy merchants... in all sorts of things" (verses 17-24). Eden is listed right along with other places that did business with Tyrus. It was an actual place and known as such at that time.

As we noticed earlier, the expression about the king of Tyrus being in Eden (Ezekiel 28:13) was probably spoken in *irony*. But since the city of Tyrus carried on trade with the country called Eden, it is not impossible that the king of Tyrus could have actually visited that country himself!

THE KING OF BABYLON

Another passage that has been applied to Satan as a heavenly angel is Isaiah 14—the chapter that mentions *Lucifer*—but which is actually a poetic description of the overthrow of the king of Babylon.

The *subject* of the prophecy was "a MAN" (verse 16), the king of Babylon; *not* an angel.

The *location* of the prophecy was the city of Babylon; *not* heaven!

The *time* of the prophecy was a few centuries B.C.; *not* something that happened before human history began!

Though the king of Babylon would attain great power, would become a ruler of nations, yet he would fall from power as other kings of the past. He would die and be "as a carcase trodden under foot...cut down to the ground, which didst weaken the *nations*" (Isaiah 14:12-19). Wording such as this can hardly describe the fall of an angel from heaven prior to human history. At that point there would have been no nations to weaken!

The king of Babylon said in his heart: "I will ascend into heaven, I will exalt my throne above the stars of God: I will sit also upon the mount of the congregation, in the sides of the north: I will ascend above the heights of the clouds; I will be like the most High" (verse 13). Such figures of speech are common in the scriptures. We read that Capernaum was "exalted to heaven," an expression that none take in the literal sense (Luke 10:15). Or notice the close parallel in wording with the prophecy about Edom: "Thus saith the Lord God concerning Edom... the pride of thine heart hath deceived thee... that saith in his heart, Who shall bring me down to the ground? Though thou exalt thyself as the eagle, and though thou set thy nest among the stars, thence will I bring thee down" (Obadiah 1:1-14).

The king of Babylon, lifted up with pride, is represented as saying he would ascend into heaven; so also was it said of Capernaum. The king of Babylon said he would exalt his throne above the stars; so was it said of Edom. Such expressions symbolized pride — pride which went before destruction. Capernaum was destroyed, Edom was destroyed, Babylon was destroyed. There is no reason to take the claim of the king of Babylon, "I will ascend into heaven," to mean he was an angel in heaven before human history began. Besides, by saying in his heart he would *ascend* into heaven, it is self-evident he was not *already* in heaven!

But what about verse 12? "How art thou fallen from heaven, O Lucifer, son of the morning!" Was not *Lucifer* the name of Satan as an angel? The Bible never says so. Isaiah 14:12 is the *only* place the word "Lucifer" appears in the Bible and this within a prophecy about the king of Babylon.

The Hebrew word is *heylel* which carries the idea of

126

Artist's concept of "Lucifer" as a fallen angel — Gustave Doré.

brightness, signifying the morning star. It has been translated "shining star" (Moffatt), "shining one" (New World, Rotherham), "star of the morning" (American Standard), "day star" (Jerusalem Bible, Amplified, Revised Version), "shining gleam" (Modern Language), etc.

It was not until about 405 A.D., when Jerome translated the Bible into Latin (the Vulgate), that the word Lucifer was used in Isaiah 14:12. Originally this word, as mentioned by the historian Pliny, was simply the term by which the ancients spoke of the morning star, rising before and introducing the light of dawn. Even a number of English words are related to the Latin word *lucifer:* lucent and translucent (shining, bright, clear), lucid (shining), luciferous (giving light), Lucite (a trade-mark for a transparent resin), lucutrate (to work by lamplight), etc. Every scholar knows that the word Lucifer, as now used, is not a correct translation of the Hebrew original.

Adam Clarke has given this comment concerning Isaiah 14:12: "Although the context speaks explicitly concerning Nebuchadnezzar, yet this has been, I know not why, applied to the chief of the fallen angels, who is most incongruously denominated *Lucifer* (the bringer of light!) an epithet as common to him as those of Satan and Devil...strange indeed. But the truth is, the text speaks nothing at all concerning Satan nor his fall, nor the occasion of that fall, but of the pride, arrogance, and fall of Nebuchadnezzar."[3]

Even though men such as Jeremiah, Ezekiel, Amos, Zechariah, and Malachi lived *after* the time of Isaiah — and were familiar with Isaiah 14 — not one of them ever taught the idea that Lucifer was the name of an angel in heaven who became the devil. It was never mentioned by Jesus or the apostles. It was not until much later that this idea developed. Weston Fields has written: "The interpretation of Isaiah 14 and Ezekiel 28, which makes these passages refer to the fall of Satan, has not been generally held during church history. The connection of Isaiah 14 with Satan was begun by Tertullian, and continued by Origen."[4] Tertullian died about 230 A.D. and Origen about 254 A.D.

Once Tertullian and Origen had promoted the teaching that Isaiah 14 referred to Satan — and later Jerome used the word Lucifer in his translation — it was only a matter of time until the two ideas would merge. In 1611, the King James translators did not translate the Hebrew *heylel*, but simply brought the word Lucifer over from Jerome's Latin version. A few years later, in 1667, John Milton issued his famous book *Paradise Lost* which depicted Lucifer as an angel who sinned and was cast out of heaven. Since then, this view has been widely believed.

SATAN AS LIGHTNING

Jesus once said to his disciples, "I beheld Satan as lightning fall from heaven" (Luke 10:18), words that are commonly linked with the Isaiah 14 passage. *If,* in other verses there was direct evidence for the belief that Satan was once an angel in heaven, we would probably include this verse as supporting evidence for that conclusion. But in the absence of any such evidence, we prefer an interpretation based on the immediate *context.*

The seventy disciples had just returned from a successful preaching mission. With joy they said: "Lord, even the devils are subject unto us through thy name" (verse 17). As the gospel was preached, as the sick were healed, as devils were cast out, Satan was losing his hold; his kingdom was losing its exalted position. Three verses before, mention is made of Capernaum which was "exalted to heaven," but which would be "thrust down to hell." This signified that Capernaum would fall from its exalted position; so also we understand verse 18 as a reference to Jesus seeing the power of Satan being broken—very quickly, as *lightning* from heaven—through his ministry and that of his disciples.

Richard Weymouth, noted Bible translator, points out in his note on this passage that the tense of the word "fall" in the King James version is correct; not "falling" or "fallen," but the aorist tense. He states: "The thought is *not* that of Milton's rebel angel ('hurled headlong flaming from the ethereal sky'), banished forever from the abode of bliss, but, rather, brought down low from the place of his pride and power."[5]

CONDEMNATION

Paul said a novice (a new convert) was not to be made a leader in the church "lest being lifted up with pride he fall into the condemnation of the devil" (1 Tim. 3:6). If a person has it already in mind that the devil was an angel, was lifted up with pride, was condemned by God, and cast out of heaven, this verse could be taken to mean that God would condemn the novice *as he did the devil*. But the more normal reading would be that the *devil* is the one that condemns—it is the condemnation *of* (or by) the devil that is meant. Proof for this is found in the very next verse: A leader "must have a good report of them which are without; lest he fall into the *reproach* and the *snare of the devil*" (verse 7). It is the devil who would place a snare (see also 2 Tim. 2:26), the devil who would cause reproach, and the devil who would condemn. All of these expressions are linked together as things that the *devil* would do—*not God*.

WAR IN HEAVEN

Revelation 12:7-10 might fit in with the idea that Satan was once in heaven and fell—*but* (as with the other passages we have examined), only if we take it out of its setting.

There was war in heaven: Michael and his angels fought against the dragon; and the dragon fought and his angels, and prevailed not; neither was their place found any more in heaven. And the great dragon was cast out, that old serpent, called the Devil, and Satan, which deceiveth the whole world: he was cast out into the earth, and his angels were cast out with him.

In this passage, John was writing *prophetically* about things that were (in his day) yet to happen. He was not recording *history* as though these things had already taken place prior to Genesis! The next verse pictures Satan as the accuser of the brethren "which accused them before our God day and night." This could not refer to a time prior to the creation of man. At that time there were no brethren to accuse!

The one who is defeated in this battle is the "dragon" — nothing is said to indicate that he was a beautiful angel who, upon being defeated, was cast down and *became* the devil. Even the strongest believers in the concept that Satan was once an angel do not generally apply this passage to a battle prior to human history.

PRE-ADAMIC POPULATION?

There are some, it should be mentioned here, who teach that Satan was an angel on a pre-Adamic earth (instead of heaven). Some go so far as to say that Eden, Babylon, and Tyrus were places on a pre-Adamic earth — with the same names as places that developed later in *human* history! By such methods of interpretation, they can easily make Lucifer the king of Babylon (a pre-Adamic city!) and have an explanation for the statement that he weakened the nations (pre-Adamic nations!).

The argument for a pre-Adamic population usually goes something like this: God told Adam and Eve to "replenish the earth" (Genesis 1:28). They were to RE-plenish, that is, RE-populate the earth. They could not RE-populate the earth if it had not been populated before! This sounds very logical — in English. The fact is, however, the word translated "replenish," *mala* (*Strong's Concordance,* 4390), means to fill or to be full. It does *not* carry the meaning of RE-fill. It is translated fill or filled about 110 times in the Bible, full 47 times, fulfill 27 times, accomplished 7 times, replenish 7 times, confirm, be at an end, be expired, gather, presume, satisfied (one or two times each), making a total of over 200 times it is used. If there is any doubt that the word means to fill, and not RE-fill, with the aid of a concordance, one can look up all of these references and see for himself how the word is used. He will be convinced that *if* there was a pre-Adamic population, it cannot be based on the word "replenish" in Genesis 1:28.

ANGELS THAT SINNED

Finally, what about the angels that sinned? We read in 2 Peter 2:4: "God spared not the angels that sinned, but cast them down to hell, and delivered them into chains of darkness"; and Jude 6 says: "The angels which kept not their first estate, but left their own habitation, he hath reserved in everlasting chains under darkness unto the judgment of the great day."

I have always understood these verses to refer to angels as spirit beings. But, it *is* true that the word translated "angels" (whether in the Old Testament or the New Testament) is the word commonly translated "messengers" and can be used of *human* beings. It is the word used to describe the spies that were protected by Rahab (James 2:25); it is used of human ambassadors, prophets, priests, and messengers of various types (1 Sam. 23:27; 2 Sam. 11:19; 1 Kings 19:2; Hag. 1:13; etc.).

Since neither verse (2 Peter 2:4; Jude 6) actually mentions "heaven," some believe the "angels" that sinned were *human* messengers and link these verses with Numbers 16. In this portion, Korah, Dathan, and Abiram, along with 250 other men, rebelled against God by rejecting the leadership of Moses. These are referred to as "princes of the assembly, famous in the congregation, men of renown" who did "minister" before the people (verses 2, 9). When judgment fell, "the ground clave asunder" and some of them "went down alive into the pit [*sheol,* the word that is also translated *grave* and *hell* in the Old Testament] and the earth closed upon them: and they perished from among the congregation." Others were consumed by "a fire from the Lord" (verses 31-35). In addition to these leaders that died, there were 14,700 of the people who died in the plague (verse 49). All of these lost, of course, what is termed their "habitation," the promised land (Num. 15:2).

Merging this information in with 2 Peter 2:4 and Jude 5, 6, then, we have the following: "The Lord, having saved the *people* out of the land of Egypt, afterward destroyed them that believed not [14,700 on this one occasion]. And the *angels* [messengers, the *leaders* of the people] that sinned, which kept not their first estate [rank], but left their own habitation [inheritance], God cast down to hell, to be reserved unto judgment."

I remain unconvinced of the correctness of this view which, obviously, has some rough edges. But, if the angels or messengers that sinned were not spirit beings, an interpretation such as this would be the most plausible. In any event, whichever view we take, it is evident that the Bible does not explain the details about when, where, or why. Just because at one point a group of angels sinned against God and fell, would not, necessarily, provide an explanation about the origin of Satan. This could only be a theory.

THE DIVINE PLAN

Since God is eternal—without beginning or end—there is no way that one book, not even the Bible, could explain all events that have transpired during what might be termed eternity past. The human mind could not comprehend it all, and some things God simply has not revealed. It does seem apparent, however, that within God's plan for man, he desired that we would worship him—not because we are forced to, or programmed as mechanical robots—but because we *choose* to worship him. I say this without in any way minimizing the work of the Holy Spirit in this choice, for salvation is of the Lord and not of ourselves

133

(John 6:44; Eph. 2:8). We are told to *choose* life (Deut. 30:19), *choose* whom we will serve (Joshua 24:15), *choose* good and refuse evil (Isaiah 7:15). If there had been only evil in the world, we would not have known good. If there had been only good, we would not have known evil. In order for us to "choose," *both good and evil had to exist on this planet at the same time.*

If it was within the divine arrangement that the system of good and the system of evil function in this world, it is not unreasonable to conclude that each system needed a leader. Since God is the leader of that which is good, another power, an opposite of God (as it were), was required. It is not impossible, then, that the devil was created *as such* from the beginning.

Jesus once said the devil "was a murderer *from the beginning*" (John 8:44). This does not fit very well with the concept that he was in the beginning a holy angel and then, later—perhaps *thousands* of years later *became* the devil. We also read that a person who commits sin "is of the devil; for the devil *sinneth from the beginning*" (1 John 3:8). This could not be rightly said of Adam. According to Genesis 2 and 3, it was not until after Adam was created, after he was placed in the garden, after he named the animals, after the woman was taken from his side, and after she listened to the serpent that Adam sinned. In a definite sense Adam was not a sinner from the beginning. But, we are told the devil was a sinner *from the beginning.* Instead of him being an angel that became the devil, if anything, the reverse would come closer to the truth: Satan seeks to transform himself *into* an angel of light to deceive (2 Cor. 11:14).

Are we saying, then, that a good God created a bad devil? Certainly the devil did not create himself. He did not "just happen." We believe that GOD created *all things.* "For by him were ALL THINGS created, that are in heaven, and that are in earth, visible and INVISIBLE, whether they be thrones, or dominions, or principalities, or powers: ALL THINGS were created by him, and for him: and he is before all things, and by him all things consist"! (Col. 1:16, 17). "ALL THINGS were made by him, and without him was not anything made that was made" (John 1:3). "I form the light, and create darkness: I make peace, and create evil: I the Lord do ALL THESE THINGS" (Isaiah 45:7).

It must be admitted, of course, that questions concerning the origin of the devil are difficult, whichever view we take. If the devil was created as an evil power in the first place, it could be argued that he would be disobeying God (which is sin) if he did not sin! On the other hand, the idea that God created a beautiful angel who later became the devil, hardly solves the problem. If God created a being which he knew would become the devil, this is not radically different than if he created him as such in the first place. If God didn't know this creature would become the devil, God would not be all-knowing. If the devil at any point was able to get one step ahead of God back then, how could we be certain he might not succeed again?

At no time did the devil ever get one step ahead of God. Nothing he has done can wreck God's ultimate purpose. God is sovereign. Even the entrance of sin into this world was no surprise to God. He knew all about it, for even *"before* the foundation of the world" he had *already* planned redemption from sin through JESUS CHRIST! (2 Tim. 1:9; 1 Peter 1:20).

*   *   *

As Apollos, who came to understand "the way of God more perfectly" (Acts 18:26), so, I believe, the information about Biblical events in this book may help us come closer

135

to understanding what *really* happened. As we may have opportunity to share these thoughts with others, let us remember to always "speak the truth in *love*" (Eph. 4:15), not being critical of those who may believe differently, knowing that "knowledge puffeth up, but charity [love] edifieth" (1 Cor. 8:1). We can be glad that salvation, the *gift* of God, is not dependent on how well we understand details about the flood, or Joshua's battle at Gibeon, or the origin of Satan! In the final analysis, it is not as important *what* we know, but *whom,* so that we can say with Paul: "I *know* WHOM I have believed, and am persuaded that he is able to keep that which I have committed unto him against that day" (2 Timothy 1:12)!

NOTES

Chapter One

1. James Strong, *Strong's Concordance of the Bible* (Nashville: Abingdon Press, reprint 1947).
2. John Whitcomb and Henry Morris, *The Genesis Flood* (Grand Rapids: Baker Book House, reprint 1973), p. 121.
3. *Ibid.*
4. *Clarke's Commentary* (Nashville: Abingdon Press), Vol. 1, p. 76; *International Standard Bible Encyclopedia* (Grand Rapids: Eerdmans, reprint 1946), Vol. 1, p. 824; *Pulpit Commentary* (New York: Funk and Wagnalls, reprint 1950), Vol. 1, p. 125.

Chapter Two

1. Jan Lever, *Creation and Evolution* (Grand Rapids: Grand Rapids International Publication, 1958), p. 17.
2. Whitcomb and Morris, *op.cit.*, p. 69.
3. James Hastings, editor, *Encyclopedia of Religion and Ethics* (New York: Charles Scribner Sons, 1928), article: "Deluge."
4. John M'Clintock and James Strong, *Biblical, Theological, and Ecclesiastical Cyclopedia* (New York: Harper and Brothers, 1894), p. 738.
5. Frank Kendig and Richard Hutton, *Life-Spans* (New York: Holt, Rinehart, and Winston, 1979).
6. Arthur Custance, *The Extent of the Flood: Doorway Papers #41* (Ottawa: Arthur Custance, 1958), pp. 19, 20.
7. *The World Almanac and Book of Facts—1982* (New York: Newspaper Enterprise Association, Inc., 1981), p. 161.

Chapter Three

1. Custance, *op. cit.*, p. 20.
2. *The Guinness Book of World Records* (New York: Sterling Publishing Co., 1983), p. 67.

3. J. Sidlow Baxter, *Explore the Book* (Grand Rapids: Zondervan Publishing House, reprint 1966), Vol. 1, pp. 41, 42.
4. Bernard Ramm, *The Christian View of Science and Scripture* (Grand Rapids: Eerdmans, 1954), pp. 244, 245.
5. M'Clintock and Strong, *op. cit.*, p. 739.
6. Ramm, *op. cit.*, p. 244.
7. Robert Jamieson, *Critical and Experimental Commentary* (Grand Rapids: Wm. B. Eerdmans Publishing Co., reprinted 1948), Vol. 1, p. 99.
8. Russell L. Mixter, *Creation and Evolution* (American Scientific Affiliation, Monograph Two, 1950), p. 15.
9. *Pulpit Commentary,* vol. 1, p. 143.

Chapter Four

1. Madeleine Miller and J. Lane Miller, *Harper's Bible Dictionary* (New York: Harper and Brothers, 1959), p. 810.
2. Whitcomb and Morris, *op. cit.*, p. 34.
3. Ramm, *op. cit.*, p. 240.
4. *International Standard Bible Encyclopedia,* Vol. 2, p. 824.
5. Ramm, *op. cit.*, p. 336.
6. Flavius Josephus, *Antiquities of the Jews* (Philadelphia: The John C. Winston Company, 1957 edition), 1, 3:6.
7. *Ibid.,* 1, 4:1.
8. *The Interpreter's Bible* (Nashville: Abington-Cokesbury Press, 1952), Vol. 1, p. 524.
9. Hastings, *op. cit.*, article: "Deluge."
10. Ramm, *op. cit.*, p. 336.
11. Whitcomb and Morris, *op. cit.*, pp. 483, 486.
12. Ramm, *op. cit.*, p. 249.
13. *Collier's Encyclopedia* (New York: Macmillan Educational Co., 1983), article: "Iraq."
14. *Ibid.,* article: "Disasters."
15. *Harper's Bible Dictionary,* article: "Flood."
16. M'Clintock and Strong, *op. cit.*, p. 740.

Chapter Five

1. Howard M. Teeple, *The Noah's Ark Nonsense,* (Evanston, Illinois: Religion and Ethics Institute, 1978), p. 104.
2. David Wallechinsky and Irving Wallace, *The People's Almanac* (Garden City, New York: Doubleday, 1975), p. 732.

3. Violet M. Cummings, *Noah's Ark: Fact or Fable* (San Diego: Creation-Science Research Center, 1972), p. 113.
4. Gordon Gaskill, "The Mystery of Noah's Ark" in *Reader's Digest,* September 1975, p. 152.
5. Floyd Bailey, *Where is Noah's Ark?* (Nashville: Abingdon, 1978).
6. *Scientific American,* July 1980, p. 77.
7. A. R. Fausset, *Expository Bible Encyclopedia* (Grand Rapids: Zondervan Publishing House), article: "Noah."
8. Epiphanius, *Panarion I,* 1:18.
9. Hippolytus, *Refutation of All Heresies,* 10:26.
10. Julius Africanus, *Chronography* 4.
11. *Christianity Today,* Sept. 12, 1969, p. 48.
12. Josephus, *op. cit.,* 1, 3:6.
13. *The New Catholic Encyclopedia* (New York: McGraw-Hill, 1967), Vol. 4, p. 742, article: "Deluge."
14. Fausset, *op. cit.,* p. 516.
15. *The Interpreter's Bible,* Vol. 1, p. 537.
16. Hastings, *op. cit.,* article: "Deluge."

Chapter Six

1. *The Jerome Biblical Commentary* (Englewood Cliffs, New Jersey: Prentice-Hall, 1968), p. 135.
2. M'Clintock and Strong, *op. cit.,* Vol. 4, pp. 1026, 1027.
3. Robert Dick Wilson, "What Does 'The Sun Stood Still' Mean?" in *Moody Monthly* (Chicago: Moody Press, October 1920).
4. *Pulpit Commentary,* vol. 7, p. 166.
5. *International Standard Bible Encyclopedia,* Vol. 1, p. 448.
6. *Ibid.,* p. 449.
7. *Ibid.,* p. 448.
8. *Wycliffe Bible Commentary* (Chicago: Moody Press, 1962), p. 218.
9. *International Standard Bible Encyclopedia,* p. 448.
10. A. Lincoln Shute, "The Battle of Beth-Horon," in *Bibliotheca Sacra,* 1927, p. 422.
11. *Pulpit Commentary,* Vol. 7, p. 166.
12. Shute, *op. cit.,* p. 430.
13. *The Wycliffe Bible Commentary,* p. 218.
14. M'Clintock and Strong, *op. cit.,* Vol. 4, pp. 1026, 1027.

15. *Pulpit Commentary,* Vol. 7, pp. 166, 167.
16. Quoted in *Lange's Commentary* (New York: Scribner's Sons, 1884), Vol. 4, p. 100.

Chapter Seven

1. Clarke, *op. cit.,* Vol. 2, p. 551.
2. *Ibid.*
3. *International Standard Bible Encyclopedia,* article: "Dial of Ahaz."
4. *Encyclopedia Americana* (Danbury, Connecticut: Grolier Inc., 1981), article: "Circle."
5. *Encyclopedia Judaica* (Jerusalem: Keter Publishing House, 1972), Vol. 15, p. 519.
6. *The Infancy* in *The Lost Books of the Bible* (Cleveland, Ohio: World Publishing Company, 1926), pp. 38-54.
7. Ralph Woodrow, *Amazing Discoveries within the Book of Books* (Palm Springs, California: Ralph Woodrow Evangelistic Association, 1979).
8. Clarke, *op. cit.,* Vol. 1, p. 760.
9. *The Interpreter's Bible,* Vol. 2, p. 567.
10. George M. Lamsa, translator, *The Holy Bible Translated from Ancient Eastern Manuscripts* (Philadelphia: A. J. Holman Company, 1961), p. 417.

Chapter Eight

1. Hal Lindsey, *Satan is Alive and Well On Planet Earth* (Grand Rapids: Zondervan, 1972), pp. 47-50.
2. *Harper's Bible Dictionary,* p. 148.
3. Clarke, *op. cit.,* Vol. 4, p. 82.
4. Weston Fields, *Unformed and Unfilled* (Phillipsburg, New Jersey: Presbyterian and Reformed Publishing Co., 1976), p. 142.
5. Richard Francis Weymouth, *The New Testament in Modern Speech* (New York: Harper and Brothers, 1929 edition), p. 166.